SPECTRUM®

Science

Grade 8

Spectrum®
An imprint of Carson-Dellosa Publishing LLC
Greensboro, North Carolina

Photo Credit: Page 22. NASA'S Earth Observing System Data and Information System (EOSDIS) through the Distributed Active Archive Center (DAAC) Alliance. Arctic Sea Ice Comparison 1979 and 2003.

Photo Credit: Page 70. NOAA Photo Library. At The Ends of The Earth Collection. Ice Core Sample. NOAA Climate Program Office, NABOS 2006 Expedition. Arctic Ocean, north of western Russia.

Photo Credit: Page 132. National Park Service Photo. Hovenweep National Monument. Hovenweep Castle. Colorado, Utah.

Spectrum®
An imprint of Carson-Dellosa Publishing LLC
P.O. Box 35665
Greensboro, NC 27425 USA

© 2015 Carson-Dellosa Publishing LLC. Except as permitted under the United States Copyright Act, no part of this publication may be reproduced, stored, or distributed in any form or by any means (mechanically, electronically, recording, etc.) without the prior written consent of Carson-Dellosa Publishing LLC. Spectrum® is an imprint of Carson-Dellosa Publishing LLC.

Printed in the USA • All rights reserved.

ISBN 978-1-4838-1172-7

07-139177811

Lesson 1.1　Scientific Reasoning

reasoning: the process of forming conclusions, judgments, or inferences based on facts or other evidence

deduction: reasoning from the general to the specific, in which a conclusion must be true because it's based on true statements

induction: reasoning that uses specific events or facts to draw more general conclusions

evidence: something that helps either prove or disprove a conclusion

theory: a statement that explains a group of facts or phenomena; most accepted theories have been repeatedly tested and can be used to make predictions about nature

hypothesis: a statement that explains a specific fact or phenomenon; a hypothesis is tested in each scientific experiment

The example of deductive reasoning that's probably more famous than any other is: Socrates is a man. All men are mortal. Therefore, Socrates is mortal.

What's the difference between deductive and inductive reasoning?

Science is about discovering the reasons why things happen in the universe, so it shouldn't be a surprise to learn that scientific knowledge is gained through **reasoning**. There's more than a single way to reason, though, and one plays a much bigger role in science than any other.

Deduction is a form of reasoning that uses broad, generalized facts to draw conclusions about specific questions or events. For example, let's say you go to bed one night, wake up at dawn, and the ground is covered in a layer of fresh snow. You also see a line of tiny footprints imprinted on the snow. Using deductive reasoning, you know an animal walked there during the night. You reach this conclusion because, **a**: animals leave footprints when they walk through snow; and **b**: the snow fell during the night; therefore, **c**: an animal walked across the snow during the night. If **a** and **b** are true, then **c** must be true.

Deduction doesn't really lead to new knowledge, though. When a more general truth is already known, deduction simply proves that more specific instances are true as well. You know that gravity causes objects to fall when they're dropped, and an apple is an object, so concluding that an apple will fall when it's dropped isn't particularly informative.

Science is mainly based on **induction**, which, in a way, is the opposite of deduction. Inductive reasoning uses specific examples to draw more general conclusions. Going back to the tracks in the snow, induction might lead you to conclude that a possum walked across the yard at night. In five years, you've never observed any animals but possums during the night. The tracks also appear to have been made by a small, four-legged animal. Therefore, it was most likely a possum that crossed the yard. Inductive reasoning leads to most likely conclusions, but there's always a chance, no matter how small, that something else is the answer.

Scientific knowledge is gained through inductive reasoning. Scientists observe specific events, whether they occur in nature or in controlled experiments. Then, based on the accumulated **evidence** from many specific observations, they draw conclusions about the world. Much of what we think of as scientific fact began as a hypothesis. A **hypothesis** is an explanation—based on background knowledge and observations—for very specific events that occur in the natural world. Hypotheses are tested in scientific experiments, and if not proven wrong, they often become the building blocks of theories. A **theory** is an explanation that applies to multiple events. In other words, a theory is a broader, more general explanation. Since science is based on induction, even the strongest hypotheses and theories have to be adjusted if new evidence appears.

Read the following examples of reasoning. Then, write **deductive** or **inductive** on the line to indicate which type of reasoning was used.

1. ___inductive___ A biologist studying chimpanzees in the wild knows that young chimps have light brown faces and older chimps have dark gray faces. Chimp 1435 has a light brown face, so the biologist reasons that it's a young chimp.

2. ___deductive___ A truck traveling from Detroit to Chicago takes the most direct route. The most direct route from Detroit to Chicago runs through Michigan City, Indiana. Before arriving in Chicago, the truck will pass through Michigan City, Indiana.

3. ___deductive___ Most nights you look outside and see light from a street lamp illuminating the sidewalk. Then, one night you look outside and the street is dark. You reason that the bulb must have burned out in the lamp.

4. ___inductive___ In the 1920s, Edwin Hubble and other astronomers made the observation that galaxies are expanding away from each other at a steady rate. Other scientists calculated the galaxies' speeds and directions of movement, and then worked backward. They reasoned that all the galaxies and the matter in them must have once been combined into a single point of matter that exploded and began the observed, expanding motion.

5. ___deductive___ Each year, Alfonse has observed the leaves on trees near his home changing colors and falling to the ground during autumn. Then, in spring, the leaves reemerge. Alfonse reasons that the same thing will happen this year as well.

Write your answers on the lines below.

6. Write your own example of deductive reasoning.

My mom always uses the stove to cook. Sometimes we eat outside food. There fore

7. Write your own example of inductive reasoning.

_____

paleontologists: scientists who study life from past geological periods

physiology: the study of the structure and makeup of organisms and how they function

In some labs, CT scans—like the kind hospitals use to do brain scans—are used on dinosaur skulls. Then, researchers use computers to create 3-D models of the insides of the skulls. This helps them figure out the size of the dinosaur's brain and can even give them information about the animal's sight or sense of smell.

An elephant's trunk is muscle and its large, floppy ears are made of cartilage, a relatively soft material. This means that the skeleton of an elephant would give no indication of two of its most recognizable features.

How do scientists figure out what dinosaurs looked like?

Do you know what dinosaurs look like? You've probably seen their images hundreds of times. Although most people could easily describe one, the truth is that no one really knows what dinosaurs looked like. The creatures that the word *dinosaur* bring to mind are actually the joint creations of **paleontologists** and artists. While they do their best to be scientifically accurate, a lot of educated guesswork is involved.

Fossils are the source of most of what is known about dinosaurs. As paleontologists unearth dinosaur bones, they must note the location of the bones in relation to one another. This information can be useful when they assemble a skeleton. It's very rare to find all the bones of an individual dinosaur. Many are washed away by water, moved by scavengers, or damaged by bacteria or the effects of weathering. Scientists look for other dinosaurs of the same species so that they can assemble a complete skeleton.

An in-depth knowledge of animal **physiology** is necessary because it can give paleontologists clues about how dinosaur bones fit together. The study of other dinosaur skeletons can also provide information, though there is no guarantee that all other dinosaur skeletons have been put together correctly.

Once a complete skeleton has been created, the next step is to determine how the muscles and tendons would have filled out the body of the dinosaur. Soft-tissue generally isn't preserved because it decays too quickly. However, soft tissues often leave microscopic marks on bones. The places where muscles were attached also leave marks. By comparing these marks to the marks on the bones of modern-day animals, paleontologists and artists can make more accurate predictions about the outward appearance of dinosaurs.

It's impossible to know what colors the dinosaurs were, but they are usually drawn in shades of brown and green, because these colors would have provided camouflage. Making this assumption requires researching the environments where dinosaurs lived. By choosing this sort of coloration, scientists also assume that dinosaurs could see in color—otherwise color camouflage wouldn't have protected them from one another.

Although there are new ways of learning about the appearance of dinosaurs, it's likely that some elements of what they looked like will always remain a mystery. Filling in the details will be left to the paleontologists who study them and the imaginations of the artists who portray them.

Write **true** or **false** next to each statement below.

1. _____true_____ Complete dinosaur skeletons are rarely found.

2. _____fake_____ The images most people have of dinosaurs were created totally from the imaginations of artists.

3. _____true_____ Imprints of soft tissues are found near most fossilized dinosaur bones.

4. _____ Dinosaur skeletons in museums are usually made from the bones of more than one dinosaur of the same species.

5. _____ There is no sure way to know what colors dinosaurs were.

Write your answers on the lines below.

6. After reading the sidebar text, you know that it isn't obvious from looking at an elephant's skeleton that it has a trunk and huge ears. What does this tell you in terms of the appearance of dinosaurs?

   _____

7. How can modern technology help scientists figure out what dinosaurs looked like?

   _____

8. Explain why the environment in which a dinosaur lived can give paleontologists a clue about its coloring.

   _____

   _____

9. If it turned out that dinosaurs were colorblind, how would this affect some assumptions scientists have made about them?

   _____

   _____

10. What information can paleontologists gain by doing comparative studies of the bones of dinosaurs and the bones of modern-day animals?

   _____

   _____

The Evolution of Ideas

fossil bed: an area of land that contains fossils

diverse: of different kinds, forms, or types

evolutionary line: the sequence of organisms that descend from one particular organism

evolutionary biologist: a scientist who studies the origins and evolution of living organisms

misinterpreting: understanding or explaining incorrectly

arthropods: the largest phylum in the Animal kingdom, it includes insects, spiders, and crustaceans

Trilobite fossils found at the Burgess Shale helped scientists date the other creatures found there to the Cambrian period, which lasted from 530 to 520 million years ago. This period in Earth's history saw a phenomenal increase in the diversity and abundance of Earth's life forms within a relatively short time.

Another of Stephen Jay Gould's debated hypotheses was that evolutionary change occurs in sudden bursts, followed by long periods of stability.

How does new knowledge change the way scientists look at old discoveries?

Around 1909, Charles Doolittle Walcott received a bit of interesting news. Canadian railroad workers were collecting "stone bugs" that they had found while cutting a path through the Rocky Mountains. Walcott was the head of the Smithsonian Institute, and a respected paleontologist, so he rushed to see what kinds of fossils had been found.

From 1910 to 1917, Walcott collected more than 65,000 specimens from the area—a massive **fossil bed** he named the *Burgess Shale*. After Walcott returned to Washington, D.C. with his fossils, he began the task of categorizing them. He didn't recognize many of the creatures, so he classified them as odd examples of organisms already known to have existed in Earth's prehistoric past. Eventually, the fossils ended up in drawers at the Smithsonian, and there they sat, mostly forgotten, for almost 50 years.

In the 1960s, Canadian scientists decided to take another look at the Burgess Shale. They discovered even more fossils, and a new study, led by Harry Whittington began. He traveled to D.C. and reexamined Walcott's forgotten fossils. Many years had passed since their discovery. A lot of new information was known about Earth's earliest life-forms and how they had evolved into the **diverse** organisms of today. Whittington and the other scientists were shocked to discover such a huge collection of creatures that looked like no other organisms they'd ever seen before.

Most fossils have an **evolutionary line** that can be traced to other creatures in the fossil record, or even to organisms that exist today. Many of the creatures in the Burgess Shale fossils, though, seemed to have appeared at just this one time in history. They didn't slowly evolve over time into other known organisms. Instead, something seemed to have happened that caused them to become extinct soon after this one appearance in the fossil record.

In his popular book, *Wonderful Life*, **evolutionary biologist** Stephen Jay Gould argued that this characteristic helped prove his idea that luck plays as much, if not more, of a role in evolution than natural selection does. Gould's book angered the scientists who were still studying the fossils. They felt that Gould was **misinterpreting** their data to support his hypothesis.

By the 1990s, paleontologists Derek Briggs and Richard Fortey had reclassified most of the unusual Burgess Shale organisms as **arthropods**. The fossilized creatures were ancient relatives of insects—not completely unique life forms that had never evolved.

Circle the letter of the best answer to each question below.

1. The creatures preserved in the Burgess Shale fossils are most closely related to modern

    a. reptiles.

    b. mammals.

    c. fish.

    d. insects.

2. The Cambrian period occurred

    a. thousands of years ago.

    b. a few million years ago.

    c. hundreds of millions of years ago.

    d. billions of years ago.

Write your answers on the lines below.

3. Further research into the Burgess Shale fossils showed that the data did not support Gould's hypothesis. Do you think this information proved that Gould was wrong? Why or why not?

    _____

    _____

4. Major museums such as the Smithsonian Institute have thousands, if not millions, of artifacts that are stored away, but not displayed. Based on what you read in this selection, why is it important for museums and other institutions to hold on to artifacts, even if they are no longer currently being studied?

    _____

    _____

5. The biggest criticisms of Gould's book didn't focus on his hypothesis; they focused on his methods. Why do you think scientists' methods of investigation need to be carefully examined by other scientists?

    _____

    _____

relative dating:
ordering events or
objects in time
without assigning
actual ages or dates

absolute dating:
determining an actual
age for an object or a
date of occurrence for
an event

radiometric dating:
a method of absolute
dating in which the
amount of a
radioactive element
that remains in a
material after it has
begun to decay is
measured

Using radiometric
dating, Earth has been
dated at 4.5 billion
years old. The planet's
oldest rocks were
formed about 3.8
billion years ago, but
meteorites in our solar
system have been
dated at 4.5 billion
years old. Earth and
the meteorites would
have formed at the
same time—with the
formation of our solar
system—so they
should be
approximately the
same age.

Dendrochronology is
the use of a tree's
growth rings to
determine the age of a
tree and what the
environmental
conditions were like
during its lifetime.

How can scientists determine the age of objects and events from Earth's past?

Antiques dealers can use style, workmanship, and materials as clues to date a piece of furniture or a vase. It's quite a bit more complex for scientists to assign an age to a fossil, a piece of rock, a tree limb, or even a geological event. Like an expert in antiques, a paleontologist or geologist will gather clues about an object. Then, he or she will use the information to determine the object's age. Over the years, methods of dating have improved and allow most materials to be dated with accuracy.

Relative dating was used before a reliable method of **absolute dating** was discovered. It allowed scientists to determine the order of events or tell whether one object was older than another. For example, using the law of superposition—one of the principles of relative dating—a geologist knows that the oldest beds of rock form the bottom layers in a series, while the most recent are on top.

When methods of absolute dating became possible, scientists could assign an actual age to objects and events, instead of just ordering them in time. **Radiometric dating**, developed after radioactivity was discovered in 1896, is one of the best-known methods. It's based on the theory that radioactive elements decay at predictable rates.

Carbon dating is frequently used to date organic remains. It's based on the fact that there is always a specific percentage of all carbon that exists as the isotope carbon-14. Those unstable carbon-14 isotopes steadily break down and turn into nitrogen-14. Other processes ensure there is always the same percentage of carbon-14. However, when the organism dies, the percentage will not stay at its stable amount. Over a period of 5,730 years, half the carbon in a dead plant, for example, will have changed to nitrogen. This is called the *half-life* of carbon-14. In another 5,730 years, half the remaining carbon will have changed to nitrogen. By measuring how much carbon-14 there is in the organic material, scientists can tell how old it is.

One problem with using carbon dating is that it's useful only to date things that are less than about 40,000 years old because carbon's half-life isn't very long. Other radioactive elements can be used for some types of dating, but like carbon, they also have limits.

One type of dating isn't superior to another. In fact, scientists generally use more than one method when possible. This allows them to double-check their conclusions and be sure that they are as accurate as possible.

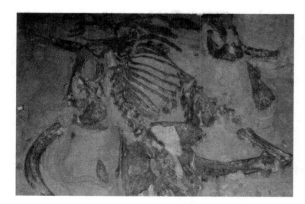

Write your answers on the lines below.

1. How could a natural event, like an earthquake, make it difficult to use the law of superposition?

   _____

2. Sam is the oldest in his group of friends. Amira is five years younger than Sam, Lea is between Sam and Amira in age, and Marcus is the youngest. Arrange the names of the friends in order from youngest to oldest.

   _____ _____ _____ _____

3. Explain whether you used absolute or relative dating in the previous item and why you were able to use one method but not the other.

   _____

   _____

4. Why would a radioactive element need to have a known rate of decay in order for it to be useful as a dating tool?

   _____

   _____

5. Why is the use of carbon-14 dating limited?

   _____

6. Describe a scenario in which a scientist might use both relative and absolute methods of dating.

   _____

   _____

   _____

Unifying Concepts and Processes

When paleontologists dated the Burgess shale fossils to the Cambrian period because trilobites were found among them, were they using relative dating or absolute dating?

   _____

The Cicadas of Summer

nymphs: insects that haven't reached full maturity; nymphs look like adults, but they are smaller, don't have fully-developed wings, and can't reproduce

molt: to shed an outer skin or covering in order to allow growth

brood: a group of young that hatch at one time

Cicada is a Latin word that means "tree cricket."

Cicadas are harmless; they don't sting or bite.

When millions of cicadas are buzzing at once, the sound can reach 90 decibels. That's loud enough to damage your hearing if you're exposed to it for too long.

Cicadas are a common treat in parts of Asia. Although they are edible, and trying a few won't hurt you, the cicadas in the U.S. may contain trace amounts of pesticides, so it's not recommended that you eat too many of them.

If cicadas emerge only once every 13 or 17 years, why do you hear them every summer?

Each summer in July and August, the steady buzz of cicadas fills the air across much of the United States. Male cicadas produce this noise in order to attract mates. When dozens of cicadas buzz at once, the sound can be loud, but when millions of them are calling out at once, the sound can be nearly deafening.

Although there are thousands of different species of cicadas, they're all members of the Cicadidae family of insects. The most common cicadas in America are in the genus *Tibicen*. They emerge from the ground as **nymphs** in July and climb into nearby trees to **molt**. The adult cicada leaves behind its old exoskeleton as it flies off to find a mate, and the empty shells remain clinging to tree trunks and branches.

For a few short weeks, the male cicada's song can be heard echoing through the trees, but soon after mating, the male cicadas die. The adult females survive a bit longer in order to lay eggs in tiny slits they've cut into tree limbs, but then they die as well. Several weeks later, the eggs hatch and the larvae that emerge fall to the ground. They burrow deep into the soil, where they'll live for the next few years by feeding on juices from tree roots. About three years later, they reemerge as nymphs, and the cycle continues.

Although *Tibicen* cicadas are more common, the *Magicicada* genus is the one that makes the news. They emerge in the millions—and sometimes even in the billions—every 13 or 17 years, depending on the **brood**. In some wooded areas, the swarms are so thick that you can quickly end up with a dozen cicadas clinging to your body. The sound can be so overwhelming that it can be difficult to hold a conversation.

Entomologists believe there are a total of 15 *Magicicada* broods that emerge in different years and in different areas scattered across the eastern U.S. In 2004, Brood X emerged after its normal 17-year absence. Covering an area from Illinois to New York, and south to Georgia, Brood X is the largest of all the broods. Red-eyed cicadas filled the air. Because *Magicicadas* emerge a little earlier than *Tibicens*, most of them had mated and died by mid-July. The forest floor was littered with millions of rotting cicada carcasses, but chemicals released by the decomposing bodies provided important nutritional elements to the soil.

Write your answers on the lines below.

1. What's the difference between *Tibicen* and *Magicicada* cicadas?

   _____

2. Explain the life cycle of a cicada.

   _____

   _____

   _____

3. How does the emergence of millions of cicadas at once benefit the environment?

   _____

4. How might the emergence of millions of cicadas at once benefit the cicadas?

   _____

5. In 2007, Brood XIII reemerged in Illinois. After weeks of news reports about the cicadas' return, people in some of the suburban areas surrounding Chicago were disappointed when no cicadas appeared in their neighborhoods. In areas like state parks, though, the air was absolutely swarming with bugs. Use the following clues to explain why you think the cicadas may have disappeared from these suburban areas.

   • Cicadas don't migrate. The adults rarely travel more than a quarter of a mile from where they first emerged as nymphs.
   • These *Magicicada* nymphs spend 17 years living several feet underground.
   • Nymphs molt in trees, and the adults lay eggs in tree branches.

   _____

   _____

   _____

What's Next?

Scientific classification is an important tool for describing and categorizing Earth's many millions of living organisms. Look in the library or online to find a list of the eight major categories, and then choose an animal to discover how it's classified scientifically.

Investigating Microorganisms

fermentation: the process in which microorganisms, especially bacteria and yeast, break down plant or animal materials

microorganisms: single-celled organisms too small to be seen by the naked eye

bacilli: rod-shaped bacteria

Edward Jenner created the first vaccine in the 1790s when he discovered that injecting patients with cowpox would immunize them from smallpox—a similar virus that could be contracted only once.

Pasteur's work with fermentation led him to the creation of the germ theory of disease—the idea that microorganisms from outside the body can cause disease within it. It took a long time for the scientific community to accept the idea. It seemed illogical to scientists that something that couldn't even be viewed without a microscope could cause damage to an organism as large as an animal or a human being.

"Where observation is concerned, chance favors only the prepared mind."
—Louis Pasteur

How did the idea that germs cause disease come about?

Louis Pasteur, a chemist and biologist, held the belief that scientific research should aid in the development and progression of industries. When beverage manufacturing plants were having problems with liquids spoiling during the mid-1800s, Pasteur used his microscope to observe the **fermentation** process. When a batch was bad, he found that other **microorganisms** had mixed with the yeast. He showed that heating liquid to around 60°C (140°F) would kill the microorganisms and sterilize the product to prevent contamination. This heating process is known as *pasteurization* and is still used today to prevent bacterial growth in milk, juice, and other beverages.

Pasteur's work with fermentation led him to research the origins of microorganisms, which he believed came out of the air. He performed a simple experiment by collecting air at different altitudes into flasks of yeast-filled liquid. The flasks had long, narrow necks that would allow air to enter but would trap dust and microorganisms. The liquid remained free of microorganisms as long as Pasteur didn't shake the flask. Once shaken, the liquid would begin to host microorganisms and turn cloudy. This confirmed his hypothesis about where germs came from, but other scientists had to be convinced that substances couldn't just produce germs on their own—an idea known as *spontaneous generation.*

With a greater understanding of the origins of germs, Pasteur set about to discover better ways to prevent diseases. He was studying chicken cholera, when he left his lab in the heat of the summer and returned to find that his cultures would no longer make the chickens sick. He grew new cultures and injected those chickens as well as a second batch. The chickens that had been previously injected with the damaged batch of cholera remained well, while the new group of birds grew sick and died. He deduced that the summer heat had made the **bacilli** noninfectious and learned that he could reproduce the effect by growing it in a warmer environment. He went on to create vaccines for rabies and for anthrax in sheep.

Louis Pasteur led the way for a new era of medicine, in which patients could anticipate a cure for their illnesses. His students and colleagues continued to isolate disease-causing bacteria and develop vaccines. Deeper understanding of these bacteria led to the development of antibiotics, which have had a major impact on modern medicine.

Circle the letter of the best answer to each question below.

1. What caused Pasteur's cholera bacteria to lose their infectious quality?

    a. fermentation

    b. heat

    c. an immunity the chickens had developed

    d. Both a and b

2. Which of the following statements is not true?

    a. Pasteur's hypothesis that germs come from the air was disproved.

    b. Pasteur used both experimentation and observation in his research.

    c. Pasteur was not the first person to create a vaccine.

    d. Chance played a role in Pasteur's discovery that heat made the cholera virus noninfectious.

3. What is spontaneous generation?

    a. the idea that microorganisms have the ability to sterilize liquids

    b. the idea that microorganisms need intense heat to reproduce

    c. the idea that substances produce germs only when microorganisms are introduced

    d. the idea that substances can produce germs on their own

Write your answers on the lines below.

4. What is the germ theory of disease, and why did it take so long to gain acceptance?

    _____

    _____

5. Reread the quote that appears in the sidebar. How do you think it applies to Pasteur's experiences when studying cholera in chickens?

    _____

    _____

6. What is pasteurization, and how is it used?

    _____

    _____

Forest Champions

girth: the measure made around a body

circumference: the measurement around a perimeter, especially that of a circle

clones: exact genetic copies of an organism

Three trees have been on the National Register of Big Trees since it was created in 1940: a giant sequoia in California's Sequoia National Park, a Rocky Mountain juniper in Utah's Cache National Forest, and a western juniper in California's Stanislaus National Forest.

"We can talk about the future, we can dream about the future. But if we really want a future, we must act."
—David Milarch, founder of The Champion Tree Project

If a tree is very tall, it can be difficult to measure its height from the ground. Using tools like a laser, a clinometer, or a relascope allow big tree hunters to get accurate measurements.

Florida has 160 champions—more than any other state.

What makes a tree a champion?

The criteria for what makes a tree a champion depend on whom you're talking to. For some, a champion tree might be a very large or ancient tree. For others, it might be the tree with the best fall foliage or the juiciest fruit. In 1940, an organization called *American Forests* began to keep records of the largest tree for each species in the United States. These trees became known as *champions*.

It can be hard to accurately compare the sizes of trees, so American Forests devised a three-part system of measurement. A tree is awarded points based on its height, **girth**, and crown. The point totals are entered into a mathematical formula, and the tree with the highest total for each species is considered the National Champion. If two trees fall within five points of one another, then they are named co-champions.

The girth of a tree is its trunk's **circumference**. The measurement is taken four-and-a-half feet from the base of the tree, and one point is awarded for each inch. The height is measured from the trunk's base to the top of the highest branch. Finally, the crown spread, or leafy, green portion of the tree, is measured. The crown can vary in size on a single tree, so the narrowest and widest parts are measured. The measurements are added together and then divided by two to get an average. To calculate the total points, the crown spread (in feet) is divided by four and then added to the height (in feet) and girth (in inches). This number will be compared only to other trees of the same species to determine the National Champion.

Although we often see trees as permanent fixtures of the landscape, there are many threats to their well-being. Fire, drought, disease, insects, acid rain, and human development can easily cut short the life of a tree. Fortunately, awareness is growing in America, and more people are taking an interest in the environment and trying to "go green." In addition, members of the Champion Tree Project gather samples from champions so that new saplings—**clones** of the parent trees—can be grown and the trees' genetic material can be preserved. The new trees are part of an archival living library—an assurance that the most amazing specimens of trees in our country will never truly be lost.

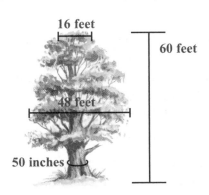

16 feet

60 feet

48 feet

50 inches

Use the measurements above to answer the questions that follow. If you need to, use a scrap sheet of paper or a calculator to find the answers.

1. How many points for girth would this tree receive? _____

2. What is the average spread of the crown? _____

3. Use the formula in the selection to determine the total number of points the tree shown above would be awarded. _____

Write your answers on the lines below.

4. Why are three elements used to determine the size of a tree, instead of just height?

    _____

5. Why do you think it's important that American Forests documents the largest trees and keeps a record over time?

    _____

    _____

6. List three threats to the health of trees in the United States.

    _____

7. Why are trees compared only to members of the same species?

    _____

What's Next?

Are there any national champions in your state? Do some research to find out. If you know of a tree that you think might be a champion, learn how to measure and nominate it.

Scientific Rights and Wrongs

subjective: depending on personal experiences and opinions

gene therapy: treatment for a disease that involves changing the patient's genes

differentiated: become specialized

therapeutic: used for medical treatment

Modern-day life support technology has raised many ethical issues. Some people believe that a patient should be kept alive as long as technology allows. Others believe that when there is no hope of the patient recovering, he or she should be removed from the machine. The issue can become even stickier when the wishes of the patient aren't known and the family has to make the decision.

An ethical issue for doctors is whether they should be required to provide care for a patient who is ill with a serious and contagious disease. Do all patients have a right to treatment? In some places, legislation has passed guaranteeing that people cannot be discriminated against because of illness.

How do we balance moral issues and scientific progress?

Ethics is the philosophy of right versus wrong. Because such views can be **subjective**, philosophers look at six main values to study an ethical situation: autonomy (freedom to make your own decisions about your life), beneficence (promoting the well-being of others), justice, nonmaleficence (not doing harm to others), veracity (truthfulness), and fidelity (keeping promises). When two or more values conflict, there is an ethical dilemma.

In science, the values of beneficence versus nonmaleficence are often at odds. Researchers struggle to balance the good that can be done by research with the harm that may come to the research subjects, or possible harmful applications of their work.

In 1990, four-year-old Ashanthi deSilva became the first patient to receive **gene therapy**. Ashanthi suffered from an immune system deficiency. Doctors took cells from Ashanthi's blood and used genetic engineering to insert the missing gene into them. This procedure cured Ashanthi.

Using gene therapy on a seriously ill child raised few ethical concerns, but some critics fear how this process could be used in the future. How do you determine which genetic "defects" need correcting, and which are simply part of what makes us unique? Could society declare certain physical traits as undesirable and then use gene therapy to eliminate them?

Cloning and stem cell research are other issues that raise ethical concerns. An embryo is made up of a group of stem cells that have not yet **differentiated** into the many types of cells that make up an organism. Scientists can extract stem cells and direct their growth to become specific types of cells that could be used to replace a person's damaged cells. Many scientists believe that the use of stem cells will lead to cures for Alzheimer's disease, Parkinson's disease, cancer, and diabetes.

One possible source of non-differentiated stem cells is cloned human embryos—except that human cloning is also an ethical dilemma. Many people feel that **therapeutic** cloning could lead to more harm than good. For example, most cloned animals are unhealthy and die young from diseases.

There is no clear answer to these ethical debates. As new scientific discoveries are made, more issues are sure to crop up. They will require that people examine both sides of the debate and come to their own decisions.

Write your answers on the lines below.

1. Although a patient is sick with a treatable illness, he decides not to accept any treatment.

   The patient has the _____ to make this choice.

2. How does the advancement of medical technology increase the number of medical ethical issues that arise? Give at least two examples.

   _____

   _____

3. What concern do some people have about the use of gene therapy?

   _____

4. Animals are commonly used in medical experimentation. In some cases, they are used to test the effects of pharmaceutical drugs. New medical procedures are also often tested on animals before they are ever used on human beings. Some people believe this is necessary, and the benefits to human beings outweigh the risks to animals. Others believe that it is inhumane and unethical to experiment on living creatures. What are your beliefs about this ethical dilemma?

   _____

   _____

   _____

5. Physicians have been taking the Hippocratic Oath for more than 2,000 years. Among other things, doctors who take the oath promise to uphold doctor-patient confidentiality. Why do you think this is an ethical issue?

   _____

6. Give an example of one pro and one con for the use of stem cells in medicine.

   _____

What's Next?

Find a copy of the Hippocratic Oath. Who was its author? What sorts of revisions have been made to it over the years?

Feeling the Heat

fossil fuels: oil, natural gas, coal, and their products; burning them releases toxic gases into the air

Greenhouse gases exist naturally on Earth. In fact, life on our planet wouldn't be possible without them because it would be covered in ice. Greenhouse gases create a sort of blanket over Earth and hold in the heat of the sun.

An increase in temperatures around the world can impact almost every aspect of life. As a result of climate changes, food supply and production are affected. Crops may have poor yields because of droughts and heat waves or because they're attacked by insects that thrive in warmer temperatures. New health issues can arise—like the increase of malaria in places it didn't use to exist. In addition, thousands of species of animals may become extinct because they cannot adapt to the changes in the environment.

The number of severe hurricanes has almost doubled in the last 30 years.

What evidence have scientists found to support the theory of climate change?

It's pretty hard to avoid hearing about climate change these days. It's a frequent topic on the evening news, and many politicians have made it a top priority. Although people debated in the past whether or not climate change exists, the vast majority of the scientific community today agrees that it is real. A panel of the world's top climate scientists believe it's more than 90% likely that climate change is caused by human activities.

Climate change is a worldwide increase in the average temperatures of Earth's oceans, atmosphere, and land. In the past 100 years, average temperatures have risen about 1.3°F. Even though this increase sounds minor, it is creating visible effects on the polar ice caps, the level of the seas, and plant and animal populations.

The warming trend on Earth began with the Industrial Age, when factories started burning large quantities of **fossil fuels** to create power. When fossil fuels are burned, they contribute to the greenhouse gases in the atmosphere, which causes temperatures to rise.

Much of the evidence for climate change comes from Earth's polar regions. Scientists analyze ice core samples for information about climate, temperature, and greenhouse gases. The samples provide a record that stretches back hundreds of thousands of years. They have shown that the amount of greenhouse gases in the atmosphere is higher today than it has been in 650,000 years.

Temperatures have increased more in the Arctic than anywhere else on Earth. Even with this slight rise in temperature, polar ice caps have begun to melt. The melting ice causes a rise in ocean levels, which then causes flooding. Because a large percentage of the world's population lives near a coastline, this rise has the potential to be extremely destructive.

Droughts and heat waves are also getting increasingly frequent, as are severe storms. Nearly 300 species of plants and animals have moved closer to the poles because of warming temperatures. We can expect to see even more effects of climate change in coming years, depending on our usage of fossil fuels.

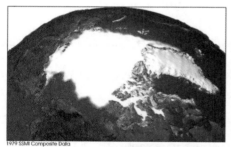
1979 SSMI Composite Data

The good news is that awareness of climate change is increasing. The evidence is growing, and people are paying attention. Do you know what you can do to make positive changes?

2003 SSMI Composite Data

Circle the letter of the best answer to the question below.

1. Ice core samples

   a. are becoming harder and harder to find.

   b. are a valuable tool in learning about the climate and greenhouse gases through history.

   c. show that levels of greenhouse gases are higher today than they've been for thousands of years.

   d. Both b and c

Write your answers on the lines below.

2. List four pieces of evidence that support the theory of climate change.

   _____

   _____

3. Explain the role of greenhouse gases in climate change.

   _____

   _____

4. Why would some species of animals need to move as a result of climate change?

   _____

5. Why do you think that some people didn't initially believe that climate change was taking place? What kinds of reasons might make people reject the idea?

   _____

   _____

What's Next?

Do some research to see how you can help stop climate change. You can follow some of the suggestions yourself, such as using less water and recycling as much as you can. You can also share some of the other items on the list with your family and see what changes you can make at home. Don't worry if you can't do them all. Remember, any positive changes you make are a step in the right direction.

Circle the letter of the best answer to each question below.

1. How do paleontologists know what color dinosaurs were?

   a. They examine pigments found in the bones.

   b. They have found small samples of skin preserved in glacial ice.

   c. They have used DNA testing to determine skin color.

   d. They don't know for sure, but they assume dinosaurs matched their environment.

2. What is pasteurization?

   a. a method of creating vaccines invented by Pasteur

   b. the use of heat to kill any microorganisms living in a substance

   c. the use of radiation to sterilize substances

   d. a method of speeding up fermentation

3. Which of the following is a cause of climate change?

   a. a decrease in greenhouse gases in the atmosphere

   b. burning coal to produce electricity

   c. rising sea levels

   d. All of the above

4. After writing *Wonderful Life*, Stephen Jay Gould was criticized by his fellow scientists

   a. because he misinterpreted the Burgess Shale fossil data.

   b. because his hypothesis was incorrect.

   c. because they thought he was arguing against natural selection.

   d. because he claimed the Burgess Shale fossils weren't real.

Write your answers on the lines below.

5. How are deductive and inductive reasoning different from one another?

   _____

   _____

6. How does a scientific hypothesis become a law?

   _____

7. What led scientists to date the Burgess Shale fossils to the Cambrian Explosion?

_____

_____

8. How are *Magicicada* broods damaged by development?

_____

_____

9. How are relative and absolute dating methods different from one another? Give one example of each method.

_____

_____

10. What three criteria are used to determine whether a tree is a National Champion?

_____   _____   _____

11. Why is gene therapy a controversial topic in medicine?

_____

12. Give three examples of evidence that support the theory of climate change.

_____

_____

Write **true** or **false** next to each statement below.

13. _____ Soft tissues leave marks on bones that can help scientists correctly assemble a dinosaur's skeleton.

14. _____ Most of the Burgess Shale fossils were of organisms related to modern fish.

15. _____ A brood is a young cicada that has just emerged from the ground.

16. _____ Carbon dating is useful only for materials that are less than 40,000 years old.

17. _____ Champion trees are cloned to preserve their genetic material.

18. _____ As long as the research will benefit human beings, scientists are free to use whatever methods are necessary to achieve their results.

Lesson 2.1   The Electro-Magnetic Connection

field: a region in space defined by the strength and direction of a force's influence

conduction: the transfer of heat or electrical energy through a substance

electromagnetic induction: the creation of an electrical current in a conductive substance when it's exposed to a changing magnetic field

The electrical current that passed from one insulated wire to the other in Faraday's experiment happened because of mutual induction. The current running through a wire creates a small, changing magnetic field around the wire. When another wire comes near enough, this changing magnetic field induces a current to flow in the second wire as well.

Nearly all the appliances in your home contain induction motors. An induction motor uses an electrical current to create a circle of changing magnetic fields that cause a rotor to spin.

Who discovered that electricity and magnetism were two aspects of the same thing?

Nineteenth-century scientist Michael Faraday made several important discoveries in chemistry, but it was his work with electricity that had the greatest impact. His interest in electricity was sparked by a series of experiments conducted by Danish **physicist** Hans Christian Oersted. In 1820, Oersted discovered a fascinating relationship between electricity and magnetism. He concluded that an electrical current running through a wire also created a magnetic **field** around the wire.

Faraday immediately began his own research. Several years later, he designed an experiment that wrapped two insulated wires around a large iron ring. When he sent an electrical current through one of the wires, he detected a current running in the other. The current couldn't have passed from one wire to the other because of **conduction**—the insulation surrounding the wires made that impossible. Faraday suspected it had something to do with the magnetic field surrounding the first wire.

Later, Faraday made a coil of wire and placed a magnet inside it. He found that when he moved the magnet back and forth, an electrical current began flowing through the wire. The same thing happened if the magnet remained still and he moved the coil back and forth. Although Faraday wasn't exactly sure why it was happening, he concluded that the changing magnetic field was causing the current to flow through the wires. He had just discovered **electromagnetic induction**.

Faraday kept experimenting, and soon he saw that a magnetic field could also have an effect on light. This discovery was the first indication that light is a form of electromagnetic energy.

About 20 years later, James Clerk Maxwell used Faraday's groundbreaking work to write a series of mathematical equations that clearly explained electromagnetic fields and their effect on matter. Maxwell's work connected the dots laid down by Faraday concerning light, electricity, and magnetism. In one of science's greatest moments, Maxwell concluded from his research that light must be a form of electromagnetic energy—a discovery that opened the door to much of the scientific research that would dominate the 20th century.

Circle the letter of the best answer to each question below.

1. What happens if a magnet is moved back and forth inside a coil of wire?

   a. The magnet becomes electrified.

   b. The coil becomes magnetized.

   c. The magnet loses its magnetism.

   d. The coil gains an electrical current.

2. The first indication that light was a form of electromagnetic energy occurred when

   a. Faraday measured the electrical current in a bolt of lightning.

   b. Maxwell measured the speed of light.

   c. Faraday saw that light could be affected by a magnetic field.

   d. Maxwell suggested that electromagnetic energy moved as waves.

Write your answers on the lines below.

3. Explain the difference between electrical conduction and electrical induction.

   _____

   _____

4. If you place a compass near an electrical current, explain what should happen and why.

   _____

   _____

Unifying Concepts and Processes

When an electrical current runs through a wire, it emits electromagnetic energy into the space that surrounds the wire. Explain why this field of energy is considered a force.

_____

_____

_____

Families of the Periodic Table

ionized: lost or gained electrons and became an ion

chemical reactivity: the relative ability of an atom or molecule to undergo a chemical reaction with another atom or molecule

compounds: substances made up of two or more elements that have bonded chemically to form molecules

semiconductors: solid substances that conduct electricity better than insulators, but not as well as conductors

inert: not chemically reactive

The total number of electrons each element increases as you move down the table, which also means the numbers of shells do. As electrons are positioned farther from the atom's nucleus, they're more easily lost. This means the elements also become more conductive as you move down the table.

How are the elements divided up to form the periodic table?

Elements in the periodic table are listed in order of their atomic numbers. These numbers indicate how many protons an atom of each element has in its nucleus. It also tells you how many electrons each atom has, as long as the atom hasn't become **ionized**.

Electrons in an atom are divided into separate atomic orbitals, or shells, surrounding the nucleus. Each orbital can hold up to a certain number of electrons before a new orbital shell is needed. Depending on the number of electrons it has, an atom might need one, or as many as seven, shells.

The horizontal rows of the table are periods. The elements listed in each period need the same number of shells to contain their electrons. For example, aluminum and argon are both in the third row, so they both need three shells.

The vertical columns of the table are groups. The elements in each group have the same number of electrons in their outermost shells. The number of electrons in the outermost shell plays a big role in determining **chemical reactivity**. Chemical bonds are formed when atoms share their outermost electrons in order to end up with full outer shells. The closer an atom is to having a full outer shell, the more readily it reacts with other substances.

The elements are also divided into families, like the following:

- Alkali metals are listed below hydrogen in column one. They have just one electron in their outermost shells, which makes them highly reactive. In nature, they're almost always part of **compounds**.

- Poor metals, including aluminum and tin, are softer than other metals, and they melt and boil at lower temperatures.

- Although most elements are considered either metals or nonmetals, the seven metalloids are a bit of both. The best-known characteristic of metalloids, like silicon, is that they're **semiconductors**.

- The noble gases in column eight have full outer shells, so they're **inert**.

- Transition metals begin in the fourth period and lie between the second and third groups. Unlike the other elements, their reactivity involves the second-to-outermost shell. The metals you know best—iron, copper, gold, silver— are transition metals.

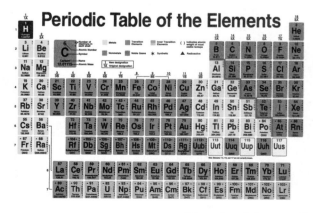

Circle the letter of the best answer to each question below.

1. Each of the elements in the same group of the periodic table

   a. has the same atomic number.

   b. has the same number of electrons.

   c. has the same number of electrons in the outermost shells.

   d. has the same number of protons in the nuclei.

2. Each of the elements in the same period of the periodic table

   a. has the same number of protons and electrons.

   b. has the same number of atomic orbitals.

   c. has the same number of electrons in each orbital.

   d. belong to the same family.

3. Any element that needs to gain or lose just one or two electrons in order to have a full outermost shell will tend to be

   a. highly reactive.

   b. a metalloid.

   c. ionized.

   d. All of the above

For the first 18 elements, the maximum number of electrons per orbital, in order, is 2, 8, and 18. For example, a silicon atom has 2 electrons filling its first shell, 8 filling the second shell, and 4 only partially filling its outermost shell—a total of 14 electrons. Use this information to list the electrons per orbital for these elements.

4. Oxygen (O): inner shell _____   outer shell _____

5. Aluminum (Al): inner shell _____   middle shell _____   outer shell _____

6. Sodium (Na): inner shell _____   middle shell_____   outer shell _____

What's Next?

The most abundant element in the universe is hydrogen. It also has the simplest atomic structure. Search for one of the many interactive periodic tables on the Internet to learn more about this unique element.

The Nature of Light

electromagnetic spectrum: the entire range of electromagnetic waves, including everything from giant radio waves to tiny gamma rays

photon: subatomic particle that carries electromagnetic energy

massless: having no mass, and therefore not affected by gravity

visible spectrum: the range of electromagnetic wavelengths detected by human sight

Light can be either an electromagnetic wave or a particle, depending on how it is being measured.

Incandescence is visible light caused by heat. Luminescence is light caused by chemical reactions or electrical energy, and therefore isn't necessarily hot. A regular light bulb that uses a filament creates light through incandescence. A fluorescent bulb creates light through luminescence.

You see it all day long, but do you really know what light is?

Light is most commonly defined as the wavelengths of electromagnetic energy that fall within a range that human eyes can detect. In science, though, the term *light* can be used more broadly for a few other wavelengths in the **electromagnetic spectrum**. UV and infrared light are the "invisible" wavelength ranges that are just outside human beings' visual capabilities. In any case, light is electromagnetic energy that travels through space in the form of waves—and it all begins at the subatomic level.

Remember, the electrons orbiting an atom's nucleus are grouped into separate shells. Electrons in the innermost shell have the least amount of energy, while electrons orbiting in the outer shells have increasing amounts of energy, depending on how far the shell is from the nucleus.

When an atom becomes energized, whether it's because of an increase in temperature or electromagnetic energy, the electrons orbiting the nucleus become energized as well. An electron that gains energy will suddenly have more energy than it should for the shell its in, so the electron will hop outward to the next shell. When the electron falls back into its original orbital shell, it releases the energy.

The tiny bit of energy released by one of these energized electrons is called a **photon**. A photon is a tiny, **massless** particle of electromagnetic energy that moves at the speed of light—because it is light. Although photons are particles, they move through space as waves—electromagnetic waves—and the more energy photons have, the shorter their wavelengths.

When matter becomes energized, it seldom releases photons at a single energy level. Instead, a wide range of electromagnetic energy waves are emitted. We see the wavelengths that fall within the **visible spectrum**, and we feel infrared radiation as heat. Although you don't see or feel them, waves of ultraviolet radiation can burn your skin, and gamma rays, with their extremely high energy levels, can even kill you.

Heat is the most common reason that photons are released from matter. As atoms become increasingly energized, they release photons with increasingly shorter wavelengths. For example, the wavelength of blue light is shorter than the wavelength of orange light, so a blue flame is much hotter than an orange flame.

Circle the letter of the best answer to each question below.

1. Which of the following statements is true?

    a. All light is electromagnetic energy.

    b. Electromagnetic energy is created only by heat.

    c. Matter emits a single, unique photon when it's heated.

    d. All of the above

2. A photon that carries more energy will _____ than a photon that carries less energy.

    a. be heavier

    b. be brighter

    c. have a shorter wavelength

    d. All of the above

3. A white light bulb emits

    a. infrared light.

    b. electromagnetic energy.

    c. photons.

    d. All of the above

Write your answer on the line below.

4. Explain the role electrons play in producing light.

    _____

Unifying Concepts and Processes

1. Radio waves are a form of electromagnetic energy. Name two things radio waves have in common with visible light.

    _____

2. According to the first law of thermodynamics, energy is neither created nor destroyed. What does this law tell you about a substance or object that is emitting light?

    _____

    _____

The Fundamental Forces

gluons: the messenger particles for the strong force; they get their name because they "glue" quarks together

messenger particles: subatomic particles that are exchanged between matter and create force

infinite: not limited by space or time

radioactive decay: the natural change of an unstable atomic nucleus into a lighter one, in which radiation is released as subatomic particles

gravitons: in theory, they are the subatomic particles responsible for gravity

Gravity keeps entire planets from drifting away from the sun and leaving the solar system, so you might wonder why it's considered weak. Drop a book and then pick it back up. The book fell because of Earth's gravitational pull, but you had no trouble overcoming the gravity of an entire planet when you picked up the book. This tells you that the force of gravity is pretty weak.

What do gravity and electricity have in common?

A force is an action or form of energy that causes matter to change speed, direction, or shape. For many centuries, people thought the universe had all sorts of different forces, but today scientists know that any change can be explained using a combination of just four fundamental forces.

- The most powerful force in the universe is the strong force. It acts on the protons inside an atom's nucleus. Protons should repel each other because they all have positive charges, but the strong force is the reason that they don't. Protons and neutrons are made up of even smaller particles called *quarks*. Quarks stick together because they exchange **gluons**. Like photons, gluons are **messenger particles** that contain energy but have no mass. The strong force is created by gluons passing back and forth between quarks. As powerful as the strong force is, it works only across extraordinarily short subatomic distances.

- The electromagnetic force is much weaker than the strong force, but it's still more powerful than the other two fundamental forces. Electromagnetism causes matter to be attracted to or repelled by other matter, but only when they both carry electrical charges. Photons are the messenger particles of electromagnetism, and unlike gluons, they have nearly **infinite** range. For example, photons emitted by a star trillions of miles from Earth still have enough force left, after traveling all that distance through space, to affect the nerves in your eyes so that you can see the star in the night sky.

- The weak force gets its name because it's very weak. This force causes certain particles to be released during **radioactive decay**. At incredibly high temperatures, the weak force and the electromagnetic force are a single force called the *electroweak force*. In the more common temperatures found throughout the universe, though, they act differently enough to be seen as two separate forces.

- Gravity is by far the weakest of the fundamental forces, but it probably has the greatest influence on matter in the universe. Gravity has nearly infinite range, and it will affect any two masses, regardless of size or electrical charge. Gravity is always attractive, though. Scientists think that gravity is caused by the exchange of messenger particles called **gravitons**, but these particles have never been detected. The exact cause of gravity remains a mystery.

Circle the letter of the best answer to each question below.

1. Which of the following is not a messenger particle?

   a. photon

   b. gluon

   c. neutron

   d. graviton

2. Roasting a marshmallow over a fire is an example of which force in action?

   a. strong

   b. weak

   c. electromagnetic

   d. gravity

Write the name of each fundamental force next to its brief description.

strong	gravity	electromagnetic	weak

3. _____ Occurs at the subatomic level; is a cause of radioactive decay

4. _____ Acts across an infinite range of distances; has very little strength; occurs between any two masses regardless of size or charge

5. _____ Occurs at the subatomic level across extremely short distances; overrides the normally repulsive action of like-charged particles

6. _____ Acts across an infinite range; occurs between any two charged masses

Write your answers on the lines below.

7. The messenger particles for the electromagnetic force are _____.

8. The messenger particles for the strong force are _____.

9. The messenger particles for gravity are most likely _____.

10. Force and energy aren't exactly the same thing, but they are closely related. Explain how.

    _____

    _____

vaporize: to change from a solid or liquid into a gas

neutral: having no electrical charge

Although the atoms drifting through space and filling the areas between galaxies and stars are extremely spread out, they are also ionized, which means they are plasmas.

Plasma screen TVs contain hundreds of thousands of tiny, individual cells. Each one contains a mixture of neon and xenon gases. The cells are connected to electrodes that excite the gases and change them into light-emitting plasmas.

A fifth state of matter, called the *Bose-Einstein condensate*, occurs when matter loses enough heat energy to begin approaching absolute zero. On Earth, these temperatures are found only in laboratory experiments. At such low temperatures, the individual atoms move so slowly that they begin clumping together into single particles.

Does a plasma TV really contain plasma?

One of the first things you learn when studying chemistry is that substances can undergo physical changes in state. They can be solids, liquids, or gases, depending on how energized the atoms and molecules have become. Although these changes occur at different temperatures depending on the substance, when enough heat is present—or absent—each substance will solidify, liquefy, or **vaporize**. These are the three best-known states because they're the ones we observe most often here on Earth. However, there's actually a fourth state that's much more common—plasma. In fact, some scientists estimate that nearly 99 percent of all matter in the universe exists as plasma.

Plasma is similar in structure to gas, but the atoms and molecules in plasma have reached such high levels of excitement that they begin to lose electrons. Gases contain **neutral** atoms, whereas some or all of the atoms in plasmas have become ionized. The positive ions and free electrons moving about in plasmas make them excellent conductors.

As the energy level in a gas increases, and it begins changing to the plasma state, every atom and molecule doesn't become ionized at once. Cooler plasmas may contain only an extremely small percentage of ions in relation to the number of atoms that are still whole. The hottest plasmas, though, have become completely ionized.

The ionized atoms in a plasma emit visible light waves. Unlike most solids, though, plasmas don't need to have reached high temperatures in order to emit light. Probably the most familiar plasma that people see every day is the one glowing inside a fluorescent light bulb. An electrical current is applied to a mixture of mercury and argon gas enclosed inside the bulb. The electricity excites the atoms and creates a plasma state that emits light. A fluorescent lamp creates light at a much cooler temperature than an incandescent light bulb, which burns brightly when a solid, metal wire has become hot enough to glow.

The aurora borealis and lightning are both examples of plasma occurring naturally in Earth's atmosphere. However, the most important plasma in the solar system is the giant, scorching ball of light and heat known as the sun. Deep in the sun's core, hydrogen atoms fuse together to form helium atoms. This creates a tremendous amount of energy that changes gases inside the sun into plasmas. In fact, all stars are plasmas energized by nuclear fusion.

Circle the letter of the best answer to each question below.

1. Plasma is

    a. an ionized gas.

    b. a glowing liquid.

    c. a solid that has become so energized it doesn't melt, but simply vaporizes.

    d. All of the above

2. The energy in a lightning bolt changes _____ into plasma.

    a. moisture in the air

    b. gases in the atmosphere

    c. dust particles

    d. electricity

3. Which of the following is an example of vaporization?

    a. gas changing into a plasma

    b. ice melting and then refreezing

    c. a puddle of spilled gasoline evaporating into the air

    d. water droplets condensing onto a window

Write your answers on the lines below.

4. Name the four most common states of matter, from least energized to most energized.

    _____   _____   _____   _____

5. Explain how the substance inside a fluorescent tube changes when an electrical charge is added to it.

    _____

    _____

Unifying Concepts and Processes

Do you think a neon light is more similar to an incandescent light or a fluorescent light? Explain how you know.

_____

_____

Making a Cabbage Juice pH Indicator

pH indicator: a chemical that changes color when it comes in contact with an acid or a base

acidic: a sour substance that has a pH of less than 7

basic: a bitter substance that has a pH of greater than 7; also referred to as *alkaline*

neutral: neither an acid nor a base; measures 7 on the pH scale

litmus paper: a commonly-used pH indicator; it turns red in acids and blue in alkaline solutions

Cabbage leaves aren't the only place anthocyanin pigment can be found. It is also found in apple skin; plums; red poppies; red onions; hibiscus flowers; cornflowers; rose, tulip, and violet petals; cherries; and grapes.

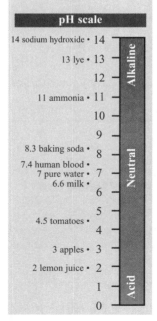

pH scale

14 sodium hydroxide •	14
13 lye •	13
	12
11 ammonia •	11
	10
	9
8.3 baking soda •	8
7.4 human blood •	
7 pure water •	7
6.6 milk •	6
	5
4.5 tomatoes •	4
3 apples •	3
2 lemon juice •	2
	1
	0

Alkaline (12–14 region), *Neutral* (around 7), *Acid* (0–6 region)

Why is cabbage juice a good indicator of a substance's pH?

Materials: a head of red cabbage, distilled water, a grater, a pot, a strainer, an eyedropper, baking soda dissolved in water, white vinegar, lemon juice, window cleaner, lemon-lime soda, antacid tablet dissolved in water, a white coffee filter, six small containers (such as clean baby food jars)

Safety Tips: Be sure to ask an adult for help. Use a potholder when removing the pot from the stove. Wear safety goggles when testing the pH of different materials. Do not mix the substances you are testing with one another.

Procedure:

- Grate up the head of cabbage and place it in a pot. Add just enough distilled water to cover the pieces of cabbage. Don't use much water, or the cabbage juice will be too diluted. Let the mixture boil for about 10 minutes, until the water turns a deep, bluish-purple color.

- Allow the contents of the pot to cool and then strain the cabbage, reserving the colored water. It will be your **pH indicator**.

- Add to each small container about a tablespoon of the substance you plan to test. Then, add several drops of cabbage water to each.

- You won't be able to get a specific pH measurement, but the color the solution turns will tell you if the substance you're testing is **acidic**, **basic**, or **neutral**. In an acidic substance, such as the vinegar, the cabbage juice will turn pink or red. In an alkaline solution, it will turn yellowish-green. In a neutral solution, it will not change color.

- You can also use cabbage water to make your own **litmus paper**. Place a white paper coffee filter in cabbage liquid that is as concentrated as possible, and give it time to soak. Remove it from the water, and allow it to dry completely. Once it has dried, you can cut it into strips and dip the strips into various solutions to test their acidity.

What's Going On: The letters *pH* stand for "potential of hydrogen." A pH indicator measures the concentration of hydrogen ions in a substance. Substances that are neutral have a pH of 7. Acids give up hydrogen ions, so they have a low pH between 0 and 6. Alkaline or basic substances (like baking soda or antacids) accept hydrogen ions and have a high pH between 8 and 14. Red cabbage leaves contain a pigment called *anthocyanin* that changes color based on the pH of its environment. By extracting this substance into a solution, you can use it as a pH indicator.

Circle the letter of the best answer to each question below.

1. What color would the cabbage solution turn if you were testing a neutral substance?

   a. red

   b. green

   c. yellow

   d. It wouldn't change color.

2. In the experiment, what purpose does boiling the cabbage in water serve?

   a. It extracts the anthocyanin pigment from the cabbage leaves.

   b. It neutralizes the anthocyanin pigment in the cabbage leaves.

   c. It changes the acidity of the cabbage.

   d. Both a and c

Write your answers on the lines below.

3. A student is performing this experiment and tests white vinegar. Using a pH indicator, she notes that the vinegar is an acid. What could she do to neutralize the vinegar? How would she be able to tell that it was neutralized?

   _____

   _____

4. In order to make your own litmus paper, you need to soak the coffee filter in concentrated cabbage water. What could you do to make sure that the liquid is concentrated?

   _____

   _____

5. Why do you think distilled water should be used to create the cabbage juice indicator? Why not use tap water?

   _____

6. Could another plant, fruit, or vegetable be used to make a pH indicator? If so, what characteristic would it need to have?

   _____

surface tension: a characteristic of liquids in which their surfaces act like they're covered by a thin, elastic film

cohesion: the force of attraction that holds together a substance's molecules; cohesion is strongest in solids, weaker in liquids, and weakest in gases

beads: forms or collects into droplets

If you're having trouble getting the needles to sit on the water's surface, place a small piece of paper towel onto the water, and then set the needle on the paper. The paper should soak up water and sink, leaving the needle at the surface. You can also rub the needle with wax.

For Part 2 of this experiment, be sure to ask an adult for help. Gather several needles of different thicknesses. Place the pot of water on a stove, and then carefully place the needles onto the water's surface. Turn on the burner. As the water warms, the needles should begin dropping to the bottom of the pot one by one. Was it the thickest or the thinnest needle that dropped first?

How can something denser than water still float?

For this experiment, you will need a wide pot, a needle, a paper towel, some thread, and water.

- Fill the pot with two inches of water. Take the needle and drop it into the pot. It will sink directly to the bottom because the needle is made of metal, and metal is much denser than water.

- Remove the needle from the water and dry it off. Now, place the needle as gently as possible onto the water's surface. This time the needle floats!

How can something denser than water float? Everything you've learned about buoyancy says it should sink. Actually, the rules of buoyancy are still valid because, technically, the needle isn't floating. It's sitting on top of a thin layer of water molecules that have created a barrier. The needle is prevented from entering the liquid because water has **surface tension**.

Surface tension is the result of a force called **cohesion**. A clear example of cohesion can be seen by pouring a small amount of water onto a table. The water doesn't keeping spreading until a thin, even coating covers the surface. The water **beads** up into a small, curved mass because cohesive forces cause the water molecules to be more attracted to each other than they are to the table's surface.

Surface tension is created by the way cohesive forces affect molecules at the water's surface. Below the surface, each molecule is attracted equally to the molecules surrounding it on all sides. There isn't an attractive force in any one direction that's stronger than the others. The water molecules at the surface, though, aren't surrounded on all sides—there are no water molecules above them. As a result, the cohesive forces aren't equally balanced, and a stronger attraction is created between the surface molecules than exists between the water molecules below the surface.

The needle doesn't break through the water's surface because the gravitational force it exerts on the water—the needle's weight—is weaker than the cohesive force that exists between the surface molecules.

Circle the letter of the best answer to the question below.

1. Water molecules below the water's surface

    a. are lighter than the molecules at the surface.

    b. are equally balanced by cohesive forces on all sides.

    c. push up on the surface molecules and create tension.

    d. are attracted most strongly to other molecules farther below the surface.

Write your answers on the lines below.

2. Why does liquid fall as drops?

    _____

3. Do you think weight or density plays a bigger role in determining whether or not an object will break surface tension? Explain your answer.

    _____

    _____

4. In Part 2 of the experiment, why did heating the water affect the surface tension?

    _____

    _____

Unifying Concepts and Properties

Many of water's special properties are due to the fact that it has polar molecules. Each water molecule has a slight negative charge on the side with hydrogen atoms, and a slight positive charge on the side with the oxygen atom. Based on this information, which of the fundamental forces causes cohesion?

_____

What's Next?

When a straw is placed into a glass of water, a tiny bit of water will climb the surface inside the straw. Adhesion is the force that causes water to cling to some surfaces. Research adhesion in an encyclopedia or online. How do both adhesion and cohesion help create capillary action, which is how plants draw water up through their roots?

The Most Common Crystal

condense: to become denser or more concentrated

buoyancy: the ability to float in a liquid or gas

crystal: a solid formed by a repeating, three-dimensional pattern of symmetrically arranged atoms or molecules

Because water becomes less dense when it freezes, it also expands. This is why you need to be careful what kind of container you use to store frozen liquids. If you've ever left a soda can in the freezer too long, you've seen what can happen.

Open containers can break, too. Because the water's surface freezes first, it seals in the water below it. As the remaining water freezes and expands, it is prevented from rising because of the frozen layer on top. It expands outward instead and can shatter a glass container.

What's so unusual about ice?

If you drop an ice cube into a glass of water, it might sink below the surface for a second, but then it will rise to the top and float. This is such a common occurrence that you probably don't give it a second thought. However, floating ice demonstrates an unusual property of water that isn't shared by many other substances.

Why is floating ice unusual, you might wonder? Start by thinking about what you already know concerning changing states of matter. When a gas cools, its molecules lose energy and begin to **condense**. The substance changes from a gaseous state to a liquid state. If temperatures continue to drop, the molecules in the liquid will become even less energetic, and they'll condense further to form a solid. In both cases, the substance becomes denser as temperatures drop and its molecules lose energy.

Now, think about what you already know concerning **buoyancy**. An object that's denser than water will sink, and an object that's less dense than water will float. Ice floats, so it has to be less dense than liquid water. In other words, the solid form of H_2O is less dense than the liquid form, which is opposite from what you'd expect based on what you've learned about changing states. So why doesn't water follow the rules?

The answer lies at the molecular level. When temperatures near 0°C (32°F), water molecules start bonding with one another to form a **crystal** structure. The hydrogen atoms of each molecule connect to the oxygen atoms of other molecules. The resulting structure creates a greater amount of space between the molecules than there was when the molecules floated freely about in a liquid state. All that extra space between the molecules is why ice is less dense than liquid water—and the reason ice floats.

This characteristic of water is good news for fish and other animals that live underwater wherever the temperatures drop to freezing. When the water in a lake, for instance, begins to freeze, the first tiny ice crystals that form remain on the surface. Eventually, a layer of floating ice will form on the water's surface, which seals in the liquid water below and keeps it from freezing. If water became more dense when it froze—the way most substances do—then the ice crystals would keep sinking to the bottom. Eventually, the entire lake would be frozen solid from top to bottom—which would be bad news for the fish.

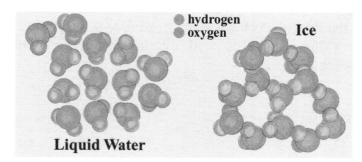

Circle the letter of the best answer to each question below.

1. H_2O molecules _____ when temperatures drop below freezing.

    a. bond

    b. form crystals

    c. create solids

    d. All of the above

2. When ice forms, the hydrogen atoms in a water molecule

    a. bond with hydrogen atoms in other water molecules.

    b. bond together and release the oxygen atom into the air.

    c. bond with the oxygen atoms in other water molecules.

    d. combine to form a single, heavier hydrogen atom.

Write your answers on the lines below.

3. Why is ice less dense than liquid water?

    _____

4. When you add ice cubes to a glass of water, the water level in the glass will rise. Once the ice melts, though, will the water level drop, rise, or stay the same? Perform this simple experiment and observe what happens. Explain in detail why you got the result you did.

    _____

    _____

    _____

Unifying Concepts and Processes

Icebergs are freshwater ice that floats in saltwater oceans. Saltwater is more dense than freshwater. Do you think more or less of an iceberg is visible above the ocean's surface compared to if the iceberg was floating in freshwater? Explain your answer.

_____

_____

Make a Density Column

density: the measurement of how much mass a substance has per unit of volume; the formula $D=M/V$ is used to find density

If you pour the liquids into the cylinder too quickly, there's a good chance they'll become mixed together. One way to make sure this doesn't happen is to tip the cylinder slightly and pour the liquids down the inside surface of the glass. This will slow them down so that they don't hit the other liquids with too much force.

You can use a wide variety of different liquids and colors to create density columns. Red, white, and blue columns, for instance, can be fun to make around the Fourth of July.

Syrup is denser than water and makes a good first layer for a density column.

How is a density column used to determine the density of solid objects?

In order to create your density column, you will need the following items: a tall, clear glass container, 250 milliliters of water with blue food coloring added, 250 milliliters of vegetable oil, 250 milliliters of mineral oil, 250 milliliters of 70% isopropyl alcohol with red food coloring added, 250 milliliters of 90% isopropyl alcohol with green food coloring added, a measuring cup that shows milliliters, a scale that measures in grams.

The first step is to determine the **density** of each liquid. Start by determining the weight of the empty measuring cup in grams. Then, add 250 milliliters of water to the cup and weigh it again. Subtract the weight of the empty measuring cup to find the weight of the water. Dividing this weight by 250 milliliters will give you the water's density in grams per milliliter. Repeat this procedure for the other five liquids to determine their densities. Record your results in the chart.

liquid	weight in grams	volume in milliliters	density
water	_____	250 ml	_____ g/ml
vegetable oil	_____	250 ml	_____ g/ml
mineral oil	_____	250 ml	_____ g/ml
70% alcohol	_____	250 ml	_____ g/ml
90% alcohol	_____	250 ml	_____ g/ml

Each liquid in a density column is denser than the one above it, so your measurements will tell you the correct order in which to add the liquids.

What you should have discovered is that water's density is 1 gram per milliliter. Your measurement may not be exactly 1 g/ml, but it should be very close. The other liquids should all have densities less than 1 g/ml. Listed in descending order of density, the liquids are water, vegetable oil, 70% alcohol, mineral oil, and 90% alcohol.

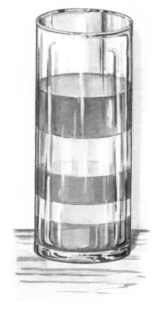

Now, measure the height of the glass container and divide the number by six. The answer will determine the height of each layer in your density column, plus a layer of empty space at the top. Starting with water, and working in order of decreasing densities, carefully add each layer of liquid. When you're finished, the colored layers should sit on top of each other without mixing.

Circle the letter of the best answer to the question below.

1. Density is a measure of

    a. mass per volume.

    b. volume per mass.

    c. the thickness of a liquid.

    d. Both a and c

Write your answers on the lines below.

2. If you were going to make a red, white, and blue density column, which liquids could you use? List them in the order you would add them to the cylinder.

    _____

3. Using what you know about buoyancy, explain why the column's liquids don't mix.

    _____

    _____

4. Do you think surface tension affects the density column, and if so, how?

    _____

    _____

5. If you dropped a penny into the density column, would it sink to the bottom of the cylinder? Explain your answer.

    _____

    _____

What's Next?

Most objects are easy enough to weigh, but determining volume can be difficult with objects that have complex shapes. In order to calculate density exactly, you need both pieces of information. However, you can get a rough estimate of an object's density by dropping it into a density column. It will be denser than the liquid it sinks to, but less dense than the liquid in the next layer down. Test different materials in your density column, like a plastic tack, a piece of cork, or a small rubber ball.

Circle the letter of the best answer to each question below.

1. Which of the following is not caused by the electromagnetic force?

    a. light

    b. gamma rays

    c. gravity

    d. radio waves

2. Alkali metals are listed in the first column of the periodic table. This tells you that

    a. they are highly reactive.

    b. they have only one electron in their outer orbital shells.

    c. their nuclei contain only one neutron.

    d. Both a and b

3. Which of the following is true about photons?

    a. Photons travel at the speed of light.

    b. Heated elements emit only one type of photon.

    c. Photons have the smallest mass of all particles.

    d. Both a and c

Write your answers on the lines below.

4. _____ is how an electrical current can pass from one substance to another, but only if the two substances are touching.

5. _____ is how one substance's changing magnetic field can create an electrical current in another substance.

6. Explain the difference between groups and periods in the periodic table of elements.

    _____

    _____

7. How are the visible spectrum and the electromagnetic spectrum similar to and different from one another?

    _____

    _____

8. What causes photons to be emitted from excited atoms?

_____

9. List the four fundamental forces in order of increasing strength.

_____   _____   _____   _____

10. Now, list the forces in order of their range of influence (two of them are equal).

_____   _____   _____ and _____

11. How is plasma different from gas?

_____

12. Name two examples of plasmas in nature, and one example of a human-made plasma.

_____   _____   _____

13. Why can cabbage, but not lettuce, be used to create a pH indicator?

_____

14. Describe the difference in molecular structure between ice and liquid water, and why it results in ice's ability to float.

_____

15. What does it mean to say that water molecules are polar?

_____

Use the words in the box to complete the sentences below.

neutral	semiconductor	cohesion	inert	gluon

16. Noble gases are _____, which means they rarely react with other matter.

17. An electrical current will travel more easily through a _____ than an insulator.

18. A _____ is a particle of energy shared between quarks.

19. A substance that is neither an acid nor a base, like pure water, is _____.

20. _____ is the force that holds the molecules of a substance together.

Lesson 3.1   Mitosis

mitosis: the process of cell division

DNA: long, complex molecules that contain the genetic information needed to construct new cells

chromatin: substance containing DNA chromosomes and proteins

centrosome: small area in a cell next to the nucleus; it controls the fibers, called *microtubules*, that play an important role in mitosis

chromosomes: long, thin structures that contain molecules of DNA and proteins

centromere: the point on the chromosomes where pairs are joined together, as well as where the pair attach to a fiber during metaphase

nuclear membrane: the membrane that encloses the contents of the nucleus and keeps them separate from the rest of the cell

cell membrane: the structure that surrounds and contains the contents of a cell

Chromosome pairs are shaped like Xs, with one chromosome on each side and the centromere at the center.

How does a cell make an exact copy of itself?

With a few exceptions, the cells of your body make duplicates of themselves at regular intervals through a process called **mitosis**, or cell division. Whether the cells play a role in muscle contraction, bone structure, kidney function, or any of the thousands of other jobs a cell might do depends on the **DNA** that was passed along during cell division. Here are the steps involved in mitosis.

- Interphase: A cell spends 90 percent of its life doing specific tasks as a muscle cell or kidney cell, for example. During interphase, the nucleus contains packed DNA, proteins called **chromatin**, and one **centrosome** outside the nucleus. As the cells gets ready for mitosis, it makes a copy of its DNA inside the nucleus. Outside the nucleus, proteins are being assembled to create a copy of the cell's centrosome.

- Prophase: The loose bundles of chromatin begin condensing to reveal identical pairs of **chromosomes**. Each X-shaped pair is connected at a single point called a **centromere**. Outside the nucleus, thin fibers connecting the two centrosomes begin growing and push them away from each other. Toward the end of the prophase, the **nuclear membrane** breaks apart, and the chromosomes drift to the center of the cell.

- Metaphase: The centrosomes are now pushed to opposite sides of the cell, and the fibers stretch between them across the entire cell. The nuclear membrane has dissolved, and the chromosome pairs have attached themselves to the fiber.

- Anaphase: Each chromosome pair breaks apart, and the two complete sets move along the fibers toward opposite sides of the cell. The fibers that aren't involved with transporting chromosomes continue to lengthen and push the centrosomes farther apart. This action begins stretching the **cell membrane**.

- Telophase: Two new nuclear membranes form around the chromosomes in each side of the cell, and the fibers continue elongating the cell.

- Cytokinesis: Now that the cell has two nuclei, each one containing a complete set of DNA, the elongated cell membrane pinches together in the middle. The two sides break apart, and cell division is complete.

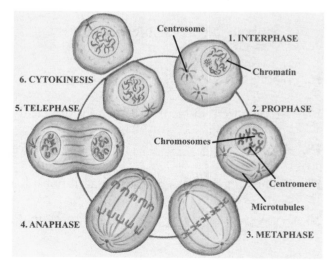

Use the words in the box to complete the sentences below.

nuclear	cell	centrosomes	cytokinesis	chromosomes
mitosis	DNA	interphase	centromere	chromatin

1. A _____ is the area of a chromosome pair that attaches to a fiber stretching across the cell during cell division.

2. Most of a cell's life is spent in _____, carrying out its specific tasks.

3. After the chromosome pairs have broken apart and been transported to opposite sides of the cell,

   two new _____ membranes form.

4. The final stage of cell division occurs during a phase called _____.

5. The fibers that grow across a cell and push it apart stretch between a pair of _____.

6. In the metaphase of _____, the nuclear membrane has completely dissolved.

7. During the prophase, bundles of _____ condense to reveal pairs of chromosomes.

8. _____ are long, complex molecules that contain genetic information.

9. After a cell has divided, the two new cells each contain an identical set of _____.

10. Centrosomes are found outside of the nucleus, but inside the _____ membrane.

Write your answer on the lines below.

11. The fibers that grow between the centrosomes are called *microtubules*. They have two important roles in mitosis. What are they?

   _____

   _____

Unifying Concepts and Properties

Healthy cells are genetically programmed to live, reproduce, and die at a steady rate. Cancer cells reproduce at a greatly increased rate, or they live longer than they're supposed to. The result is a mass of cells, called a *tumor*, which can interfere with the body's normal, healthy functions. Which part of a cell's structure do you think would most likely be abnormal in order for the cell to be cancerous? Why?

   _____

The Amazing, Changeable Brain

fixed: stable and unchanging

neuroplasticity: the ability of the brain to physically change its structure and function in response to experiences and thoughts

meditation: the act of concentrating on one's breathing or repeating a word or phrase to achieve a higher level of awareness

A study was done examining the brains of Tibetan monks who had spent as much as 10,000 hours in **meditation**. Their brain activity was compared to that of a control group who had just learned to meditate. The results of brain scans showed that the monks had a large increase in a type of high-frequency brain activity when meditating, while the control group had only a slight increase. The study found that meditation might even result in permanent changes to areas of the brain—another example of the power of thoughts to physically alter the brain.

Does the human brain have the ability to physically change and grow?

It used to be widely believed that the structure of the brain wasn't changeable. Even though human beings keep learning new things throughout their lives, it was thought that the brains of adults are essentially **fixed**. New research, however, has shown that these ideas are incorrect. The study of **neuroplasticity** is helping people become more fully aware of the brain's potential.

Neuroplasticity refers to the ability of the brain to physically change in response to experiences and thoughts. Harvard researchers performed an experiment in which they had volunteers practice playing a short piece of music on the piano for two hours a day. After five days, the researchers found that the section of the brain responsible for the motion of the fingers had grown. These findings, while not groundbreaking, supported what other recent research had found—the brain, like muscles in your arms, can grow when it gets a workout.

In the second part of the experiment, the new volunteers did not physically play the piano. Instead, they were told to imagine that they were practicing the piece of music. They didn't actually move their fingers; they just thought about how their fingers should move. When the researchers hooked up the subjects to the machines, they found that the same part of the brain that had grown in the first group also grew in the second group. Just the power of thought had changed the structure of their brains.

An awareness of the brain's ability to change and grow is important for everyone, but especially those who experience a head injury or stroke. Even if portions of the brain are damaged, other parts of the brain can take over and perform new functions. This can also be observed in people who are blind or deaf. For example, the parts of the brain devoted to sight can find a new purpose and be used for hearing or remembering. These studies show that the brain is able to rewire itself based on the way it is used.

There are better reasons today than ever before to exercise your brain. Keeping your body fit can be achieved by running or biking or lifting weights. Keeping your brain fit also involves challenging it and giving it a workout—by learning new things, doing logic puzzles or math problems, and practicing things you already know how to do. There's no telling what your brain can achieve with a little work.

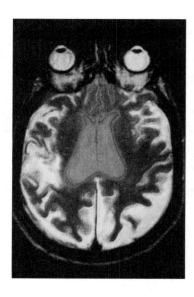

Write **true** or **false** next to each statement below.

1. _____ Meditation has no effect on brain activity.

2. _____ Mental challenges, like learning a new language or solving a puzzle, are a form of exercise for the brain.

3. _____ Research shows that if part of the brain is damaged, no other part can do its job.

4. _____ The structure of the brain is changeable, but the way the parts function is not.

5. _____ The parts of the brain involved in hearing might be different in someone who is deaf than in someone who can hear.

Write your answers on the lines below.

6. How were the experimental and control groups different in the meditation study?

_____

7. Why was it necessary to have a control group?

_____

8. Why is the discovery of neuroplasticity significant?

_____

_____

9. Sometimes, when a person has lost a limb, he or she can still feel sensations of the missing limb. Using what you've learned about neuroplasticity, explain why a person who is touched on the face might feel the touch on a "phantom," or missing, limb.

_____

_____

10. What part of the Harvard experiment's results did the researchers find surprising? What could they infer from the results?

_____

_____

The Incredible Shrinking Potato Experiment

permeable: capable of being passed through

solutions: mixtures in which particles of one or more solutes are distributed equally throughout another substance, called the solvent

solutes: the substances that are dissolved into another substance to create a solution

Both diffusion and osmosis occur because they follow the second law of thermodynamics—entropy.

Reverse osmosis uses force to move a solvent through a semi-permeable membrane in the opposite direction in which it would flow naturally. The solvent passes through the membrane, but the solutes are left behind. Instead of ending up with two solutions that have equal concentrations, reverse osmosis produces one extremely concentrated solution, as well as a solvent that has no solutes.

What's the difference between diffusion and osmosis?

Cell membranes are selectively **permeable**, which means that certain molecules can pass right through them, while other molecules are blocked. Two processes that move food, water, and waste molecules through the cell membrane are diffusion and osmosis. Diffusion is the movement of molecules from areas where they are highly concentrated into areas with lower concentrations. When a higher concentration of molecules exists outside the cell, diffusion carries them through the cell membrane in order to increase the concentration of these molecules inside the cell.

One important aspect of diffusion is that it acts separately on each type of matter. This is helpful when a cell has a high concentration of waste molecules inside, while at the same time there is a high concentration of food molecules outside. Even though the **solutions** on both sides of the membrane are highly concentrated, they contain different **solutes**. Diffusion allows the waste to flow out at the same time the food flows in.

Osmosis is similar to diffusion, but it refers specifically to the movement of water molecules. Water will always flow from an area with fewer solutes toward an area with more solutes until the solutions in both areas are equally concentrated. The following experiment shows osmosis in action.

- Mix two tablespoons of sugar into 4 oz. of water (Solution A).
- Mix two teaspoons of salt into 4 oz. of water (Solution B).
- Slice three very thin, one-inch square pieces from a skinned potato.
- Place each in a shallow dish and label it.
- Pour just enough of Solution A to cover the potato slice in Dish A.
- Pour just enough of Solution B to cover the potato slice in Dish B.
- Pour just enough plain water to cover the potato slice in Dish C.
- Let the slices soak for 30 minutes, and then remove them.
- Measure the potato slices to see if they have changed sizes.

Solutions A and B have high concentrations of solutes—greater than the water and starch mixture in the potato. Osmosis causes water to move out of the potato slices and into the solutions in the dishes. The loss of water should have caused the slices in Dishes A and B to shrink.

The slice in Dish C should have gotten bigger. The plain water has almost no solutes, so osmosis causes the water to flow into the potato.

Circle the letter of the best answer to each question below.

1. According to the selection, diffusion plays a role in

   a. cell division.

   b. transporting food and waste.

   c. the creation of proteins.

   d. All of the above

2. In diffusion, molecules move from areas of _____ concentration to areas of

   _____ concentration.

   a. high; low

   b. low; high

   c. no; some

   d. complete; high

Write your answers on the lines below.

3. Diffusion involves the movement of _____, while osmosis involves the movement

   of _____.

4. Explain in detail why the potato slice in Dish B shrank.

   _____

   _____

5. Explain in detail why the potato slice in Dish C swelled.

   _____

   _____

What's Next?

The following experiment can help you determine approximately how concentrated the solution is in a potato or a carrot. First, fill each of eight cups with four ounces of water, measuring carefully and labeling the cups 1 through 8. Then, add one teaspoon of sugar to Cup 1, two teaspoons to Cup 2, and so on. Each teaspoon adds about 4 percent of solute to the solvent, so Cup 1 will have a 4 percent solution, and Cup 8 will have a 32 percent solution. Next, cut eight thin slices of potato or carrot. It's important that the slices be as nearly identical as possible. Place the slices in shallow dishes labeled 1 through 8, and then pour just enough of each solution to cover the slice in the dish with the same number. After 30 minutes, check the slices. Which slices shrank, which ones grew, and which one changed the least?

Smells Great!

olfactory epithelium: a membrane in the nasal cavity made up of receptors that sense odors

neurons: nerve cells

cilia: very small hair-like projections on nasal neurons

putrid: rotten

The senses of smell and taste are closely linked. A stuffy nose can make food taste much less flavorful, because about 75% of what you interpret as taste comes from your sense of smell. Your taste buds recognize things that are sweet, sour, bitter, and salty—the rest of the flavors you detect are odors.

The sense of smell is key to the survival of most animals. An acute sense of smell can warn an animal of danger, alert it to a source of food, and help it find and choose a mate. Olfaction allows animals to recognize one another and to tell friend from foe.

Human beings can distinguish between 4,000 and 10,000 different odor molecules.

How important is our sense of smell?

Your sense of smell can communicate all sorts of information to your brain. Even with your eyes closed, you'd know whether you were standing in a locker room, a bakery, or a gas station. Every time you breathe, air flows into your nostrils and over the **olfactory epithelium**—a small membrane located on the roof of the nasal cavity, below the brain and behind the bridge of the nose. Millions of olfactory **neurons** are located in this epithelium. Between 8 and 20 tiny hair-like **cilia** project from the end of each neuron. The millions of receptors in these cilia are sensitive to odors.

Research shows that there are seven different types of receptors, which respond to seven different categories of scents, including peppermint, floral, and **putrid**. The molecules of each different odor have a particular shape. They bind with specific cells in the nose, like a key fitting into a lock. When these receptors are stimulated by an odor, a message is sent from the olfactory nerve to the olfactory bulb. From there, signals are sent on to other parts of the brain where they are interpreted. It sounds like a lengthy chain reaction, but it all takes place in almost no time at all.

The ability to detect odors has practical uses for human beings. For example, a smell can alert you that a food has gone bad or that there is a gas leak in the house. Odors can also communicate something that you've learned through experience—that it's time to wake up because you can smell your dad's coffee brewing, for example. Positive associations we have with scents can also bring us pleasure. The smell of roses might remind you of your grandmother's garden, or the odor of chlorine might make you remember playing at the pool. This occurs in part because smells are transmitted to the limbic system, which includes the parts of the brain that are linked to memory and emotion.

In 2004, olfactory researchers Richard Axel and Linda Buck won the Nobel Prize for their discovery of a family of about 1,000 genes that are responsible for approximately the same number of different types of olfactory receptors. They showed that the receptor cells are highly specialized instead of being receptive to a variety of odors. Their work, which was considered a breakthrough in the science of olfaction, has brought us one step closer to understanding the mysteries of the human body.

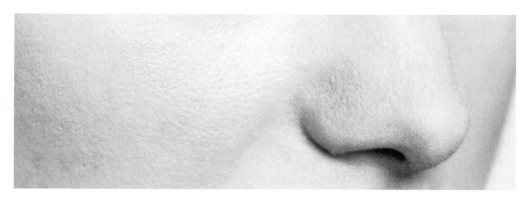

Use the words in the box to complete the sentences below.

olfaction	genes	molecules	nasal cavity	cilia

1. Tiny hair-like _____ on the ends of nasal neurons contain millions of receptors.

2. _____ describes the sense of smell or the act of smelling.

3. Human beings can tell the difference between thousands of types of odor _____.

4. Richard Axel and Linda Buck studied the _____ that shape olfactory receptors.

5. The _____ lies between the brain and the nose.

Write your answers on the lines below.

6. Give an example of a positive association you have with a particular smell. What role does your limbic system play in this association?

   _____

   _____

7. What purpose does olfaction serve in animals?

   _____

8. Explain the link between the sense of taste and the sense of smell.

   _____

   _____

Unifying Concepts and Processes

Do you think that sense of smell is more or less important for modern human beings than our earliest ancestors? Do you think our smelling abilities have changed over time? Explain.

   _____

What's Next?

Choose a partner and perform a series of experiments. Have one partner close his or her eyes while the other provides samples to sniff. Use spices, fruits and vegetables, flowers, dryer sheets, aftershave, toothpaste, vinegar, and so on. You can also have your partner sample foods with his or her eyes closed. With a plugged nose, can your partner tell the difference between an apple and a potato? Compare your results with other pairs.

Keeping an Eye on Frogs

indicator species: a species that is sensitive to changes in the environment and can serve as a warning when an ecosystem is in trouble

porous: able to absorb liquids

invasive species: a nonnative species whose introduction often causes changes to existing populations of plants and animals

In the 1960s, the sharp decline of peregrine falcons served as a warning that something was wrong in the environment. It turned out that the use of harmful pesticides, particularly DDT, was causing the falcon eggs to be very fragile. In 1972, DDT was banned because of its potential to harm the environment, wildlife, and human beings.

Beetles, spotted owls, pileated woodpeckers, Atlantic puffins, lichens (a type of fungus), and fish are all common indicator species for their habitats.

What can scientists learn from frogs about the state of the environment?

Historically, coal miners brought a canary into the mines with them because canaries are more sensitive to toxic gases than human beings. If the bird showed signs of distress, the miner would immediately leave the mine. In nature, plants and animals that are extra sensitive to their environments play the same role. These **indicator species** can provide warning signals to scientists about the health of an ecosystem.

Frogs, a common indicator species, spend their lives on land and in the water, so they are exposed to problems in both environments. In addition, they have **porous** skin and eggs, which makes them very sensitive to changes in their environment. In 2004, the Global Amphibian Assessment (GAA) did a study of the nearly 6,000 species of amphibians in the world. The assessment revealed that there were declines in the populations of 43 percent of the species. In addition, about one-third of amphibian species were found to be in danger of extinction.

One way to evaluate the health of a species is by observing its breeding behavior. Amphibians breed at certain times of year, depending on cues they get from the environment. Changes in the climate, due to causes like global warming, can alter their breeding patterns. They can also be affected by other extremes in weather, such as droughts, flooding, and early frosts.

Loss of habitat is the single greatest threat to amphibians, followed by pollution, fires, and **invasive species**. However, there are still many unknowns about what is causing the population changes. It's not happening only in areas that experts categorize as high-risk. The GAA found that amphibians around the world—in wetlands, prairies, deserts, and forests— were in decline. Amphibians have been a part of the world's ecosystems since the Devonian Period more than 400 million years ago, and yet a combination of factors in today's world is seriously threatening them.

Researchers believe that a variety of causes are at work. They think that additive causes—the combined effects of two or more factors—may be to blame for the drop in numbers. It's the responsibility of human beings to pay attention to the warning signs that our global ecosystems are out of balance and to try determine what we can do to remedy the problems.

Write **true** or **false** next to each statement below.

1. _____ The numbers of amphibians are declining only in high-risk areas of the world.

2. _____ Many amphibian species are threatened, but none have recently become extinct.

3. _____ The health of falcon populations in the 1960s indicated that pesticide use was harming the environment.

4. _____ Amphibians have been a part of life on Earth for only about 4 million years.

5. _____ Birds and fish are frequently used as indicator species.

Write your answers on the lines below.

6. Reread the last sentence of the selection. Do you agree with it? Why or why not?

   _____

   _____

7. Explain in detail why amphibians are useful as an indicator species.

   _____

   _____

8. What can scientists learn by observing the breeding behavior of amphibians?

   _____

   _____

9. What does it mean to say that additive causes are responsible for the decline in the number of amphibians?

   _____

   _____

Unifying Concepts and Processes

Explain what role inductive reasoning has in the study of indicator species.

_____

The Drive to Survive

natural selection: the process by which organisms that are best suited to their environments pass along their beneficial traits to future generations

fittest: a quality that allows animals to survive and reproduce successfully; the strongest, fastest, biggest animals of a species aren't always the fittest—any characteristic that allows members of a species to survive longer, find mates more quickly, and produce more offspring, is a trait that will be passed along to future generations through natural selection

Artificial selection occurs when farmers and breeders choose plants or animals with desirable characteristics and breed them. For example, they may choose to cultivate a tomato plant that bears extra large fruit or a cow that produces great quantities of milk. This is considered artificial selection since people, not nature, are doing the selecting.

How do certain characteristics evolve in a species over time?

The naturalist Charles Darwin spent a great deal of time studying the wildlife on the Galápagos Islands. Many plants and animals there are unique because of the islands' isolated position in the Pacific Ocean. As a result of his research, Darwin arrived at a theory he called **natural selection**.

Darwin based his theory on his observation of the large population of island finches. He believed that the different species had all evolved from the same ancestor. There was amazing variety, however, in the beaks of the 13 species of island finches. Some were perfect for cracking seeds, while others could be used to pull insects from tree branches. Darwin concluded that the birds had evolved traits that were best suited to the environment of the island on which they lived. This theory was one of Darwin's greatest contributions to science, and the finches illustrated it perfectly.

The drives to survive and to reproduce are two strong motivations for animals. The animals that are most successful—the ones that are healthiest, live the longest, and have the greatest number of offspring—are said to be the **fittest**. You may have heard the expression "survival of the fittest." Organisms that are best suited to their environments survive, reproduce, and pass along these beneficial traits to future generations. Less useful traits may disappear altogether as a species of animal evolves.

The gypsy moth is an example of a species that experienced relatively quick natural selection. Most of the gypsy moths in London before the Industrial Revolution were light gray, which allowed them to camouflage themselves and avoid being eaten by predators. Some moths were dark gray—an unfavorable characteristic because it made them more visible. Once the Industrial Revolution began, everything in London became covered with a dark layer of soot. Suddenly, the light-colored moths stood out against the dark background and the dark gray moths were better hidden. Through the process of natural selection, the dark moths, which now had better rates of survival and reproduced more successfully, became the majority.

Natural selection can be caused by human activity, as it was in the case of the gypsy moths and the pollution. It can also be the result of an event in nature, like a drought that causes a change in diet for an animal. Whatever the cause, the end results are species that continue to evolve, striving to give the best possible chances of survival to future generations.

Circle the letter of the best answer to each question below.

1. Which of the following is an example of artificial selection?

   a. A farmer breeds a species of sheep that quickly grows a new coat after it is shorn.

   b. A species of finch develops a long, pointy beak in response to competition with a bird that eats the same seeds the finch does.

   c. A beetle evolves with light brown wings that blend into leaves on the forest floor.

   d. A species of fish evolves whose eggs can survive in extremely cold waters.

2. What caused a change in color of the majority of London's gypsy moths?

   a. The soot from pollution turned them dark gray.

   b. Natural selection occurred.

   c. The pollution killed the light gray moths.

   d. Biologists haven't yet determined the cause.

Write your answers on the lines below.

3. What does *survival of the fittest* mean?

   _____

4. How do Darwin's finches illustrate the theory of natural selection?

   _____

   _____

5. Give one example of a natural event and a human activity not mentioned in the selection that could cause natural selection to take place.

   _____

Unifying Concepts and Processes

How could the introduction of an invasive species to an ecosystem cause natural selection to take place in a native species? Be specific.

_____

_____

_____

catalyst: a substance that increases the speed of chemical reactions

larvae: the young form of an insect before it develops into its adult form

regenerate: to grow a new limb

synchronized: occurring at the same time

Cypridinas are a clam-like creature about the size of a tomato seed that can shoot a bioluminescent cloud into the water. During World War II, Japanese soldiers carried a powder made from dried *Cypridinas*. They could moisten the powder and use the glow to read a map or even put some on the backs of their uniforms to be able to spot their fellow soldiers in the dark.

Most marine bioluminescence is blue because its wavelength transmits the farthest in water. In addition, many marine organisms are sensitive only to blue light.

What is bioluminescence, and how is it used by different organisms?

On a warm summer night, tiny flashes of light fill the air. The firefly's glow is the result of a process called *bioluminescence*—a chemical reaction which produces light in a living organism. The reaction involves the chemical *luciferin*, a **catalyst** called *luciferase*, and oxygen. A standard light bulb wastes about 90% of its energy in the form of heat, while only 10% is used to produce light. Bioluminescence generates a light that gives off almost no heat.

Organisms use bioluminescence to find or attract prey, to defend against predators, and to communicate with others of their species. In New Zealand, glowworms use bioluminescence to catch their prey. Glowworms are actually the **larvae** of a type of fly. They live in tubes attached to the ceilings of caves or under overhanging rocks. Flying insects are attracted to the glowing threads hanging down from the tubes and become entangled.

The brittle star uses bioluminescence for self defense. A relative of the starfish, the brittle star lives in burrows on the ocean floor but leaves its long, thin arms sticking out. If a predator attacks the arms, they flash. If the attack continues, one of the arms breaks off and slithers away from the brittle star. The body of the brittle star can then **regenerate** a new arm.

Bioluminescent flashes are also used for communication. Male fireflies flash in order to attract females. The females reply with flashing to alert the males to their location. Different species of fireflies actually flash in different patterns. Some fireflies in Southeast Asia use **synchronized** flashing. The males gather in trees in large numbers and begin flashing on and off all together. This allows the females to find them in the thick vegetation.

In general, plants are not bioluminescent, but there are a few exceptions. Some species of fungi can cause pieces of wood to glow. The glowing wood is commonly referred to as *foxfire* or *candlewood*. Dinoflagellates, a type of single-celled marine algae (not technically a plant), are also bioluminescent. When a large number of dinoflagellates are concentrated near the surface of the ocean, they can make the water glow blue. They are sensitive to pressure on their cell walls and glow when they are disturbed. This serves as a defense, because the light they produce when a predator is nearby can draw other, larger predators, which may consume the predators that originally threatened them.

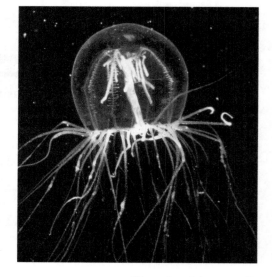

Circle the letter of the best answer to the question below.

1. What causes dinoflagellates to glow?

   a. the presence of a predator

   b. any movement that places pressure on their cell walls

   c. high concentrations of salt in the water

   d. Both a and b

Write your answers on the lines below.

2. How is the light produced by bioluminescence different from the light produced by a light bulb? Why do you think this difference exists?

   _____

   _____

   _____

3. What three components need to exist in order for bioluminescence to occur?

   _____   _____   _____

4. Bioluminescence is sometimes used to attract and sometimes to repel. Give one example of each use.

   _____

   _____

   _____

5. Why would plants and animals evolve over time to have characteristics like bioluminescence?

   _____

   _____

   _____

Life at the Edge of the Seas

erosion: the movement of rock and soil by sources such as wind, water, and ice

vacuole: a compartment that contains fluid

detritus: debris formed from decaying plants and animals

The purpose of marshes has long been misunderstood. For many years, they were used as dumping areas because they smelled like rotten eggs. Many countries dredged marshes to create deeper shipping channels to accommodate larger ships. In some locations, developers drained the water and filled the marshes with soil to create oceanfront property for commercial and residential purposes. About 50 percent of Earth's marshes have been drained and destroyed. Venice; New Orleans; Washington, D.C: and almost all of the Netherlands are built on reclaimed land.

What lives in a saltwater marsh?

Saltwater marshes can be found along coastlines where the land meets the sea. They have almost no trees or shrubs, and the water is very shallow. Most of the marshlands in the United States are along the coastlines of the Atlantic Ocean and the Gulf of Mexico. Saltwater marshes help to protect land from **erosion** due to the ocean tides that cycle in and out two times a day. These marshlands can prevent flooding, shield an area from severe weather, and filter and clean the water that passes through the marsh. The water comes and goes from the marsh throughout the day with the tides, sweeping away dead plant life and bringing in fresh nutrients.

Many plants cannot thrive in salt water, but some have adapted in order to survive. Because large trees cannot grow in most salt marshlands, the marshes receive enormous amounts of sunshine that make them hospitable to plants like tall grasses. Cordgrass actually removes salt as it filters water through its leaves. Pickleweed does not excrete the salt but stores it in a **vacuole**. When the vacuole cannot hold any more salt, it dies off. Blue-green algae also live in salt marshes and blossom in its sunny, shallow environment.

While they are teeming with life, salt marshes generally do not offer a habitat for large animals like the alligator. The ecosystem, however, is full of small creatures, like crabs, hiding in the muddy ground and birds nesting in the tall grasses. Oysters, fish, clams, and terrapins can also be found burrowing in the muddy soils of the marshlands.

The plant life in a marsh is extremely thick. It produces an important food source known as **detritus**, which is eaten by small fish, shrimp, mussels, and worms. Larger birds, fish, and crabs that are higher up on the food chain feed on the smaller animals that eat the detritus. Marshes also offer a nursery for newborn birds, fish, and crabs. The tall grasses and abundant supply of food provide a safe place for young animals to hide and eat, while giving the adults an opportunity to hunt.

Many organizations and communities are working to preserve and protect salt marshes. New developments are limited or banned in these areas, and barriers are created in some places to keep the marshes from being eroded. With a little help from their human neighbors, salt marshes can continue to protect the coastline and provide habitats for diverse populations of plants and animals.

Write **true** or **false** next to each statement below.

1. _____ Some marshes have been filled with soil to prevent erosion.

2. _____ Altering salt marshes will affect the land near coastlines.

3. _____ Less than one-quarter of Earth's marshlands still exist.

4. _____ Most species of plants thrive in the sunny, salty environment of salt marshes.

5. _____ Salt marshes are populated mostly by birds and small marine animals.

Write your answers on the lines below.

6. Give one example of a plant that lives in a saltwater marsh and explain how it has adapted to life there.

   _____

7. There is not great diversity in the plant life that exists in salt marshes. Why do you think this is?

   _____

8. What protection do saltwater marshes offer coastlines?

   _____

   _____

9. Why do marshes make an ideal nursery for young animals?

   _____

10. Aside from salinity (saltiness), what is one way in which saltwater marshes differ from fresh water marshes?

    _____

11. How has the way in which human beings use and treat marshes changed in recent years? Use specific examples to explain.

    _____

    _____

    _____

Sounds of the Wild

bioacoustician: the science or study of biology and acoustics

biophony: the sounds of nature; a combination of the words *biotic* meaning "caused by living organisms" and the root *-phon*, which means "sound."

sound niches: the tendency of animals to make sounds at different pitches and degrees of loudness to ensure they can be heard by others of their species

bandwidth: range of frequencies

soundscapes: environments or landscapes created by sound

Even the oceans aren't free of noise pollution. Motor boats, jet skis, and ships' sonar create enough noise to interfere with the communication and breeding habits of marine mammals.

Frogs and toads vocalize as a group so that predators can't locate them individually. The noise of airplanes can throw them off, and before they can get back on track and begin chirping in harmony again, they can become a meal for birds and other predators.

Are the sounds of nature disappearing?

Go outside, close your eyes, and listen to the sounds just before dawn on a spring morning or at twilight in summer. Depending on where you live, you're likely to hear a variety of chirps, buzzing, clicking, and humming. The sounds of the birds, insects, and frogs you hear are probably in competition with the sounds of human civilization—slamming car doors, radios, sirens, a passing train, a plane overhead, or just the background hum of traffic. In the modern world, it's getting harder and harder to find the pure sounds of nature without any human-related interference.

Bernie Krause, a **bioacoustician**, is on a quest to map the sounds of nature, which he calls **biophony**. During his 40 years of seeking out and recording these sounds, Krause has developed ideas about **sound niches**. We know that many animals rely heavily on their sense of hearing and their ability to communicate to others of the same species through sound. Krause has proposed that the various species of animals in an ecosystem occupy different sound niches in order to make sure that they can be heard.

This sharing of the natural sound landscape occurs out of necessity. Animals need to hear and be heard in order to survive. The sounds they make can communicate warnings of danger, the location of food, and the marking of territory, as well as play a role in mating rituals. If the sounds of all creatures existed at the same **bandwidth**, it would be impossible to distinguish one from another. Because of competition for sound space, animals are forced to find a unique and unoccupied sound niche to survive.

Krause has recorded sound environments all over the world. He uses specialized computer equipment to create visual maps of the sounds he records. Using the printouts, Krause can point out the audio "signature" of each type of animal. Currently, he has more than 3,500 hours of pure, natural **soundscapes**. He hopes to create a library of sound, partly to raise people's awareness of something that needs to be protected.

Already, many of the soundscapes that Krause has recorded have disappeared. Sometimes, loss of habitat is to blame, while in other places, the sounds of human civilization block the sounds of nature. Without a doubt, noise pollution is here to stay. That's why human beings need to work to preserve some of the world's remaining quiet spaces—for ourselves and for the animals trying to make themselves heard.

Circle the letter of the best answer to the question below.

1. Which of the following is not an example of biophony?

   a. the late-night hooting of a pair of owls

   b. the buzzing of cicadas on a summer afternoon

   c. the hum of an air-conditioner

   d. the screech of monkeys in a rainforest

Write your answers on the lines below.

2. Why does Bernie Krause record and preserve soundscapes?

   _____

   _____

3. What information can Krause get by printing out visual maps of the soundscapes he records?

   _____

4. In your own words, explain the concept of sound niches.

   _____

   _____

5. What can cause a soundscape to disappear?

   _____

6. Why is human-created noise pollution a problem for animals? Give at least two examples.

   _____

   _____

Unifying Concepts and Processes

According to Krause, animals have to compete for sound space, as well as for food and territory. Using what you've learned about natural selection, explain how this might take place.

_____

_____

Circle the letter of the best answer to each question below.

1. An indicator species

   a. tells scientists what other types of animals can be found in an area.

   b. is the same thing as an invasive species.

   c. provides scientists with signals about the health of an ecosystem.

   d. is the top predator in an ecosystem.

2. Which of the following is not a function of saltwater marshes?

   a. to offer a safe habitat for young animals

   b. to remove the salt and create fresh water habitats for plants and animals

   c. to prevent flooding

   d. to shield coastlines from severe storms

3. The finches of the Galápagos Islands

   a. evolved different types of beaks that were suited for eating different types of foods.

   b. were slowly becoming extinct when Darwin was conducting his research there.

   c. evolved from different ancestors instead of one ancestor as Darwin believed.

   d. did not support Darwin's ideas about natural selection.

Write your answers on the lines below.

4. What is neuroplasticity, and why was its discovery significant?

   _____

   _____

5. Give two examples of the use of smell in human beings and two examples in animals.

   _____

   _____

6. How are the senses of taste and smell linked?

   _____

7. What attributes do amphibians have that make them a useful indicator species?

   _____

8. Number the following steps of mitosis in the correct order:

    _____ The cell membrane pinches in the middle and divides the cell into two pieces.

    _____ Each identical set of chromosomes moves toward opposite sides of the cell.

    _____ Two new nuclear membranes form.

    _____ Chromatin condense to reveal pairs of chromosomes.

    _____ The nuclear membrane breaks apart.

    _____ Centrosomes have been pushed to opposite sides of the cell.

Write your answers on the lines below.

9. Explain Bernie Krause's ideas about the purpose of sound niches in nature.

    _____

    _____

10. What uses does bioluminescence have for animals? Give one specific example of a luminescent animal and how it uses this feature.

    _____

    _____

11. Explain how the gypsy moth illustrated the idea of survival of the fittest in London around the beginning of the Industrial Revolution.

    _____

    _____

Underline the correct answer from the two choices you are given.

12. New research indicates that the brains of adult human beings are (fixed, changeable).

13. A cell spends the majority of its life in (interphase, cytokinesis).

14. (Osmosis, Diffusion) is when the solvent in a solution with low concentration flows toward a solution with high concentration.

15. Cilia are hair-like structures that contain odor-sensitive (neurons, receptors).

16. Breeding a species of plant that is resistant to disease is an example of (natural, artificial) selection.

Mid-Test

Write **true** or **false** next to each statement below.

1. _____ Walcott classified the Burgess Shale fossils as arthropods soon after he found them.

2. _____ Temperatures in the Arctic have risen more than anywhere else due to global warming.

3. _____ Atoms that are closest to having full outer shells are most likely to react.

4. _____ Scientists have detected massless particles called *gravitons* that are responsible for the gravitational force.

5. _____ Water becomes denser when it freezes, but it also expands.

6. _____ People can distinguish between about 20,000 different odor molecules.

7. _____ Like a light bulb, bioluminescence generates most of its energy in the form of heat.

8. _____ Natural selection can be triggered by human activity or an event in nature.

Use the words in the box to complete the sentences below.

physiology	semi-permeable	photons	chromosomes	plasmas
cilia	centromeres	girth	messenger particles	spontaneous

9. A champion tree's height, _____, and crown are measured and awarded points.

10. Paleontologists need an understanding of animal _____ in order to reconstruct dinosaur skeletons.

11. Energized electrons emit _____ when they jump between orbital shells.

12. The fundamental forces are created when _____ are exchanged between matter.

13. _____ are created when the atoms in gases become ionized.

14. In the early stages of mitosis, pairs of _____ are connected at points

    called _____.

15. Cell membranes are _____.

16. _____ are hair-like structures that project from the ends of nasal neurons.

17. Pasteur's germ theory of disease was in opposition to scientists who believed in the

_____ generation of microorganisms in substances.

Write your answers on the lines below.

18. Why do scientists use as many methods as possible when dating an artifact?

_____

19. A scientist notices that a Magicicada brood doesn't appear in an area where it had appeared 17 years

earlier. She uses _____ reasoning to conclude that the construction of a new
neighborhood 12 years earlier had destroyed the nymphs living underground.

20. How are greenhouse gases both helpful and harmful to life on Earth?

_____

_____

21. What happened when Faraday moved a magnet back and forth inside a coil of wire?

_____

22. Why are the noble gases inert?

_____

23. Why does water pool or puddle on a flat surface instead of spreading out evenly?

_____

24. Water molecules form a _____ structure when they solidify.

25. What is neuroplasticity?

_____

26. Explain diffusion.

_____

27. How did peregrine falcons serve as an indicator species in the 1960s?

_____

| Lesson 4.1 | Predicting the Future |

How do meteorologists know what kind of weather is in store for us?

There are a variety of ways to predict the weather, but they all begin with making observations about current conditions—learning what the weather is before predicting what it will be. Weather forecasting involves gathering data from several sources, analyzing it, and making predictions about future conditions. Information is gathered from the observations of people on the ground, satellites, **Doppler radar**, weather balloons, ships, and planes.

In numerical weather prediction (NWP), computers are used to predict changes in the weather. The data that was gathered from a variety of sources is fed into computer systems that create maps of weather conditions. Using mathematical formulas, the computers predict how the weather will change over time. Meteorologists use this information to make their forecasts. This is why you might encounter different forecasts, depending on which channel you watch on TV. The experience and skill of the forecaster comes into play as the data he or she receives is **interpreted**.

The persistence method of forecasting is the simplest. It assumes that current conditions will not change. If it is 65°F and mostly sunny outside today, according to the persistence method, it will be 65°F and mostly sunny tomorrow. This system is most effective in places that have relatively unchangeable weather at certain times of year, or when weather systems are moving very slowly.

The trends method of forecasting involves using current information about pressure systems and fronts to make short-term predictions. For example, a meteorologist might be watching a cold front make its way across the country on a satellite image. By calculating the distance the front has traveled in a specific amount of time, he or she can make an estimate of when it will be arriving in a certain area.

Forecasting the weather isn't always an exact science. Judgement and interpretation play a part, and there is always an element of unpredictability. No matter how skillful meteorologists are and how advanced technology becomes, Mother Nature is still capable of surprising us now and then.

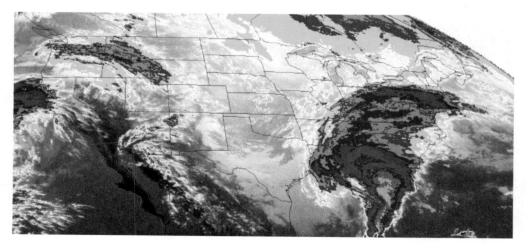

Doppler radar: a meteorological tool that measures radio waves reflected from objects in the atmosphere, such as raindrops and snowflakes; the frequency with which the waves are reflected gives meteorologists information about the movement and progress of a storm

interpreted: explained or came to a conclusion using available information

Although 10-day forecasts are available, their accuracy is limited. Five days is generally the accepted length of time for making accurate predictions about the weather. This is largely because small changes in atmospheric conditions are difficult to detect and have the potential to quickly develop into larger changes that affect weather conditions.

Weather satellites are useful tools for meteorologists because they provide a big picture of atmospheric conditions around the world. The sensors pick up on reflected light and infrared waves to gather information about weather systems, cloud formation and movement, and temperature.

Circle the letter of the best answer to each question below.

1. A snowstorm is located 140 miles away from your town. It's moving at a speed of 35 miles per hour. According to the trends method of forecasting, when will it arrive?

   a. in about 4 hours

   b. in about 2 hours

   c. in about 45 minutes

   d. Not enough information is given.

2. According to the persistence method of forecasting, if it is partly cloudy with a high of 78°F on Tuesday, what will the weather be like on Thursday?

   a. partly cloudy but much cooler

   b. sunny and 78°F

   c. the same as it was on Tuesday

   d. stormy

3. Which of the following statements is true?

   a. Doppler radar and weather satellites detect reflected electromagnetic waves to gather information.

   b. In recent years, weather satellites have been replaced by Doppler radar.

   c. Doppler radar uses the frequency with which radio waves are reflected to produce information about storm systems.

   d. Both a and c

Write your answers on the lines below.

4. Why is interpretation an important part of meteorology?

   _____

   _____

5. Why is the persistence method of forecasting limited?

   _____

6. What role does observation play in weather forecasting?

   _____

   _____

Drilling for History

ice sheet: a massive, thick covering of glacial ice; the Antarctic ice sheet is the largest mass of ice on Earth, and it contains more than 60 percent of Earth's fresh water

EPICA: acronym for the *European Project for Ice Coring in Antarctica*

glacials: the coldest periods during ice ages, when glaciers extend from the poles to cover large portions of Earth

interglacials: the warmest periods during ice ages, lasting somewhere between 10,000 and 30,000 years

According to ice core analysis, Earth's atmosphere contains more carbon dioxide today than it has in the last 800,000 years, and levels have risen at a faster rate than ever before.

Some ice cores have also been taken from the tops of Earth's tallest mountains. However, global warming is melting these once-permanent features, and a race is on to get samples before it's too late.

What can scientists learn from ice samples taken from the frozen polar regions?

On the barren, frozen continent of Antarctica, a group of scientists worked for nearly 10 years—from 1996 to 2004—to complete a single task. They bored a single, narrow hole straight down through the thick **ice sheet** and removed long, cylindrical pieces of ice, one after another, until they had a series of them stretching more than a mile and a half. The **EPICA** ice core is still the longest one ever removed from anywhere on Earth. It contains over 750,000 years of historical information about Earth's climate.

Ice cores contain surprisingly precise information about temperatures and other atmospheric conditions that occurred in Earth's past. Like the rings inside tree trunks that were created with each year's new growth, ice cores contain layers that were created with each season's snowfall. The winter snow that falls on polar regions is dense and hard compared to the fluffier snow that falls during summer. Ice cores contain alternating shades of dark, dense layers created by winter snows and light layers created by summer snows. One light and one dark layer combine to show a single year in Earth's past. The layers in an ice core that are nearest to Earth's surface came from more recent years, and the layers become older the deeper they go.

As new layers of snow accumulate, they compress the lower layers and trap air and particles from the atmosphere into the snow. Scientists can analyze each layer for its chemical content to find great amounts of information about Earth's atmospheric conditions in the past. Temperature and humidity levels can be determined by how much of certain chemicals are found. The presence or absence of other chemicals can tell scientists how high sea levels were, how much carbon dioxide was in the air, or what the sun's activity was at the time. Ash found in a layer can even indicate that a volcano erupted somewhere in the world.

The EPICA ice core revealed that Earth has experienced eight **glacials** during the last 800,000 years, with warmer periods, called **interglacials**, occurring every 100,000 years or so. Human civilization arose during the most recent interval of warm weather, and scientists estimate that this current interglacial should last about another 15,000 years. However, an increase in greenhouse gases is reversing what should be a long period of cooling off, and average temperatures are rising instead. Is the next glacial period simply on hold, or has this natural cycle been interrupted for good?

Circle the letter of the best answer to each question below.

1. The EPICA ice core revealed that

    a. Earth's climate has remained remarkably stable for nearly a million years.

    b. carbon dioxide levels were highly toxic half a million years ago.

    c. Earth has experienced eight ice ages during the last 800,000 years.

    d. Both b and c

2. The different layers in an ice core are visible because

    a. the snow that falls during winter is different from the snow that falls in summer.

    b. the ice freezes at different temperatures from one year to the next.

    c. strong winds that blow only in winter leave obvious marks on the polar ice.

    d. each summer the top layer of snow melts and creates a visible line in the ice core.

Write your answers on the lines below.

3. Why do ice cores taken from polar regions contain much older information about Earth's climate than ice cores taken from mountaintops?

    _____

4. How do gases and particles get trapped in the different layers in an ice core?

    _____

    _____

5. The oldest layers in an ice core are thinner and harder to distinguish from one another compared to the more recent layers. Why do you think this is?

    _____

    _____

Unifying Concepts and Processes

One of the most important steps in analyzing data taken from an ice core is to compare it with data taken from another ice core that came from somewhere far away. Why do think this comparison is important?

_____

_____

Under Pressure

What causes geysers to form, and why do they erupt?

A column of boiling hot water and steam shoots from the ground with incredible force. It rises up several hundred feet into the air, and just a few minutes later, it disappears, leaving behind only silence and a steamy puddle of water. **Geysers** are one of nature's most spectacular tricks. Because conditions need to be just right for a geyser to form, most of the world's 1,000 or so geysers are located in only three countries—the United States, New Zealand, and Iceland. More than half are found in Yellowstone National Park.

A geyser is a hot spring that periodically erupts into a column of steam and boiling water. Some geysers erupt on a predictable schedule. Yellowstone's Old Faithful, for example, erupts every 30 to 90 minutes. Others erupt more or less frequently, often on an unpredictable schedule.

The conditions that are necessary for a geyser to exist are a source of heat, a good supply of water, and a particular type of underground "plumbing." The water that gushes out of an erupting geyser is actually precipitation that seeped into the ground and made its way down through layers of sand, soil, gravel, and rock. Geysers are found near areas of volcanic activity. When the **groundwater** reaches layers of **magma**, or heated rock, deep below the surface, it begins to boil. Some of the water turns to steam and mixes with the cooler water that lies closer to the surface, causing it to eventually reach the boiling point as well. The deeper water is even hotter now—well above the boiling point—but it is stable because of the pressure exerted on it by the cooler water above it.

More and more steam bubbles rise. This steam and hot water would just gently bubble to the surface the way they do in a hot spring if it weren't for the underground plumbing unique to geysers. Somewhere near the surface, there must be a constriction, or a place where the water and steam cannot easily pass through. Some of the water squeezes through this narrow passage. As it does, it decreases the pressure deeper underground. This change in pressure leads to an explosion of steam and water. When the temperature drops to below boiling or all the water is used up, the eruption dies down.

As groundwater begins to refill the geyser's plumbing, the cycle repeats itself, and the next spectacular eruption prepares to take place.

---

geysers: hot springs that periodically erupt into a column of steam and boiling water

groundwater: water that lies below Earth's surface

magma: molten rock that lies below Earth's surface; it is heated by Earth's intense internal pressure and temperature

Most geyser fields contain a type of volcanic rock called *rhyolite* or other rock that is high in silica. These rocks are watertight and pressure tight, which is why they are perfect for the formation of geysers.

Geothermal energy is produced by harnessing the energy of Earth's natural heat. This alternative energy source needs an abundant supply of water and volcanic heat, just as geysers do. When geothermal energy plants are located near geysers, they can sap the water supply and cause the geysers to become inactive.

Old Faithful spouts between 10 and 12 thousand gallons of water at each eruption.

Circle the letter of the best answer to the question below.

1. Why are geothermal energy sites and geysers often located in the same areas?

   a. Geothermal energy plants use the energy that geysers produce to create electricity.

   b. Both need a large supply of water and volcanic heat.

   c. Geysers make volcanic heat more readily available to geothermal energy plants.

   d. Both a and b

Write your answers on the lines below.

2. What three conditions form the right environment for a geyser to exist?

   _____

3. What is the source of the water that erupts from a geyser?

   _____

4. What effect can geothermal energy sites have on geysers?

   _____

   _____

5. In the sidebar text, it says that rhyolite is an ideal type of rock for geysers because it is watertight and pressure tight. Why do you think this type of rock, compared to something more porous, is found in geyser fields?

   _____

   _____

6. What is constriction, and what role does it play in the eruption of a geyser?

   _____

   _____

7. What do you think affects the frequency with which geysers erupt?

   _____

   _____

The Mighty Mississippi

tributaries: streams or rivers that feed into a larger river or lake

channels: paths for the water of rivers, streams, and other waterways

estuary: the place where a body of fresh water meets and mixes with a body of salt water

sediment: particles of rocks carried by the movement of wind, water, or ice

river delta: a triangular-shaped landform created where the mouth of a river flows into another body of water

alluvium: deposits of mud, sand, and soil collected at the mouth of a river

The ever-changing path of the river can cause problems for towns built along its banks. Kaskaskia, Illinois, used to be on the east side of the Mississippi River. The river formed a new channel, and Kaskaskia is now on the west side.

How was the United States' largest river formed, and how does it continue to change?

Running 2,340 miles, the Mississippi River system—which includes the Mississippi River and its **tributaries**—is the longest and largest river in North America. It originates at Lake Itasca in northwestern Minnesota, where it starts as a small stream that is only a few feet deep. As it flows south, it collects rainwater and runoff from snow, and accumulates sediment along the way. Tributary rivers like the Minnesota, Illinois, Missouri, Ohio, and Arkansas join the Mississippi River to form one large river. The main function of the Mississippi is to drain most of the water located between the Rocky and Appalachian Mountains.

The Upper Mississippi, north of Cairo, Illinois, cuts through hilly terrain. Fifteen thousand years ago, the melting of the Wisconsin glacier formed **channels**. As the water flowed faster, it carved high, rocky outcrops along the river, called *bluffs*. The Lower Mississippi flows through much flatter lands, is deeper, carries more water, and has a more powerful current.

The Mississippi has not always been as long as it is now. Tens of thousands of years ago, the Gulf of Mexico extended all the way north to Cairo, and the river ended there. The area was an **estuary** where the river dumped **sediment** into the sea and created more land. As more land extended to the south, so did the river.

It takes approximately 90 days for the water from Lake Itasca to complete its journey to the Gulf of Mexico. The mouth of the river is located south of New Orleans in a **river delta**. The Mississippi delta was formed more than 8,000 years ago when sea levels rose and the glaciers retreated. The river deposited **alluvium** and created the shallow, marshy coastline of Louisiana. At the delta, the river fans out into hundreds of small streams, called *distributaries*, which remove water from the river. The delta helps absorb the impact from severe weather and is a defense against flooding.

Unlike many rivers of the world, the Mississippi does not follow a straight path, but meanders and curves along the route. At times, the river curves so much that it almost appears to double back on itself. The rapid current forces the Mississippi to be on a constant course to change its path. Over decades, the river can shift its path by forming a faster channel to the south. Levees have been built to control the path of the river and are used to prevent flooding and stop a drastic change of course.

Use the words in the box to complete the sentences below.

tributaries	meandering	delta	glaciers	estuary

1. Instead of following a straight course, the Mississippi is know for its _____ path.

2. A(n) _____ is where a body of fresh water and a body of salt water meet and mix.

3. Smaller rivers or streams that feed a larger river are called _____.

4. Channels of the Mississippi River were carved out by the movement of _____.

5. A(n) _____ is a triangle-shaped landform located at the mouth of a river.

Write your answers on the lines below.

6. What is one way in which human beings try to control the flow of the Mississippi?

   _____

7. Why do you think it's necessary for human beings to try to keep the course of the river from changing too much?

   _____

8. How does the Mississippi change in size from its origins as a small stream at Lake Itasca?

   _____

   _____

9. How do the upper and lower parts of the Mississippi River differ from one another?

   _____

   _____

10. Explain how the Mississippi delta and the coastline of Louisiana formed.

   _____

   _____

11. What purpose does the Mississippi delta serve?

   _____

Recycling Rocks

geological time scale: used by geologists and other scientists to discuss the timing of and relationships between events that have occurred during the entirety of Earth's 4.5-billion-year existence

tectonic plates: pieces of Earth's crust that move in relation to each other

minerals: solid, inorganic elements or compounds that have crystalline structures and contain only a single element or compound

precipitation: in chemistry, it's the process by which a solid substance is separated from a solution

Earth recycles its rocks, so it's difficult to determine the exact age of the planet. However, geologists using radiometric dating have found 3.5 billion-year-old rocks on each of Earth's continents. However, the oldest rocks were found in northwestern Canada and date back almost 4 billion years.

What makes one rock different from another?

Something as solid as rock seems like a permanent part of Earth's structure, but rocks move and change through a cycle similar to the water or oxygen cycles. However, the rock cycle takes place on a **geological time scale**.

The main "engines" of the rock cycle are Earth's **tectonic plates**. The slow, continuous motion carries rocks deep below the surface, where intense heat turns them to magma. Eventually, the rocks solidify because magma cools as it moves back toward the surface. Magma can also ooze or erupt onto the surface through volcanoes or thermal vents.

Earth's plates can move solidified rocks back to the surface, where they are exposed to wind, water, and chemicals in the atmosphere. Weathering slowly breaks rocks down into smaller and smaller pieces. Erosion carries these small pieces away as sediment and deposits them in layers that form much of Earth's crust. The rocks in these layers can become compacted and reform into larger rocks again. Here are the three main categories used to describe rocks in various stages of the cycle:

- Igneous rocks are formed when magma cools and solidifies. When this process happens slowly below ground, intrusive rocks are formed. They contain large pieces of **minerals** that can be easily identified. Extrusive rocks are formed when magma reaches Earth's surface and cools rapidly. They're usually smooth, glossy, and a single color.

- Sedimentary rocks are formed when layers of smaller rocks are compressed to form larger solids. Rocks that have been exposed to weathering create sediment that moves to new locations because of erosion. As layers of sediment accumulate, the weight pressing down on the lowest layers compresses the sediment and forms sedimentary rock. Clastic rocks, like sandstone, consist of pieces of other rocks. Biogenic rocks, like coal, occur when the remains of living organisms are compacted along with the pieces of rock. Chemical sedimentary rocks form because of **precipitation**. Water flowing across rocks picks up tiny bits of minerals and moves them to a new location. As the water evaporates, it leaves the minerals behind.

- Metamorphic rocks begin as either igneous or sedimentary rocks that are carried deep below the surface. The temperatures are high enough to melt rock, but the high pressure doesn't allow matter to expand. Instead, the rock becomes much more compact and extremely dense.

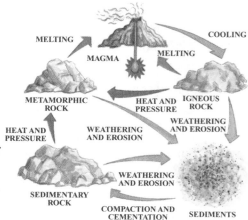

Circle the letter of the best answer to the question below.

1. When magma cools, it forms

   a. igneous rock.

   b. sedimentary rock.

   c. metamorphic rock.

   d. All of the above

Write your answers on the lines below.

2. Metamorphic rock is ___dense/compacted___ than other forms of rock.

3. What do biogenic rocks contain that makes them unique?
   ___Are made up through the remains of living organisms___

4. Describe one difference between intrusive rocks and extrusive rocks.
   ___Intrusive=below grand   extrusive=close to grand___

5. What two processes move rocks around the planet?   *erosion and movement of tectonic plates*
   ___Weathering___   ___erosion___

6. Explain the role weathering plays in the rock cycle.
   ___Rocks eventually break up into tiny pieces and are moved to other places and become different types of rock___

Unifying Concepts and Processes

Irrigation, dams, pollution, and deforestation are just a few of the ways human beings have affected Earth's water cycle. Human beings have also had an impact on the oxygen cycle by increasing the amount carbon dioxide in Earth's atmosphere. Do you think human beings are having an effect on the rock cycle? Explain your answer.
___Yes, because they are destroying rocks and such to build big things.___

What's Next?

Do some research to discover how geologists designate the different time periods in Earth's ancient past.

crust: the solid, outermost layer of Earth

strait: a narrow channel connecting two large bodies of water

Fossils of ancient sea creatures have been found high in the mountains of the Himalayas in Tibet and the Caucasus Mountains in Russia. Geologists consider these fossils as evidence that the Paleo-Tethys ocean floor moved north, collided with Laurasia, and formed these Asian mountain ranges.

The Black, Caspian, and Aral Seas are also considered remnants of the much larger Tethys Sea.

The saltiest sea on Earth is the Dead Sea between Israel and Jordan. It's nearly nine times as salty as the oceans.

The Mediterranean Sea is important to human history, but what's its geological history?

About 250 million years ago, all of Earth's land was combined into a supercontinent called *Pangaea*. The massive Panthalassic Ocean covered most of the remainder of Earth's surface, but nestled inside the curved shape of Pangaea was another, smaller ocean—the Paleo-Tethys. It was enclosed on three sides, but to the east it mixed with the waters of the much larger ocean. At the Paleo-Tethys's southern end sat the Tethys Sea.

Today, Earth's **crust** is broken into separate tectonic plates, and it was no different then. As the plates slowly ground past, over, and under each other, they broke up the single supercontinent into separate pieces. The plate that formed most of the Paleo-Tethys's ocean floor rose as it was shoved north, and this large body of water slowly disappeared. At the same time, the plate underneath the Tethys Sea made its way west. After 50 million years, the Tethys Sea's western movement had split Pangaea into two smaller continents—Laurasia to the north and Gondwana to the south.

Eventually, these continents broke up as well and formed several landmasses that were carried across the planet by the movement of tectonic plates. As these lands separated, the Tethys Sea grew much larger. Then, about 70 million years ago, the landmasses that formed Africa, Asia, and Europe began closing in on each other. Trapped between them was the Tethys Sea. As these modern continents moved into the positions we're familiar with today, the sea became completely enclosed. The largest remaining portion of this once-gigantic, ancient body of water is the Mediterranean Sea.

Surrounded almost completely by land, the Mediterranean mixes with the Atlantic Ocean only through the narrow **Strait** of Gibraltar at its western-most point. This characteristic makes the Mediterranean saltier than the ocean. When water evaporates, the salt in the water becomes more concentrated, and the limited access to another, larger body of water means the Mediterranean remains saltier.

The Mediterranean Sea also marks the place where the Eurasian and African tectonic plates meet. Like most plate boundaries, the Mediterranean is a location for geological activity, like earthquakes and volcanoes. As Earth's plates continue to move, the Mediterranean Sea won't remain the same forever. It may disappear all together, or it may spread out to once again become an entire ocean.

Circle the letter of the best answer to each question below.

1. All of Earth's land was once part of a single continent called

   a. Laurasia.

   b. Tethys.

   c. Gondwana.

   d. Pangaea.

2. The Mediterranean Sea is the largest remnant of what ancient body of water?

   a. the Pangaea Ocean

   b. the Panthalassic Ocean

   c. the Tethys Sea

   d. the Laurasian Sea

Write your answers on the lines below.

3. Why do Earth's continents change shape and move around the planet?

   _____

   _____

4. Explain why the water in the Mediterranean Sea is saltier than water in the oceans.

   _____

   _____

5. Why does the Mediterranean have so many volcanoes and earthquakes?

   _____

Unifying Concepts and Processes

People who swim in the Dead Sea usually comment on how easy it is to float in the water. Why is it easier to float in the water there than other places? [Hint: Remember what you've learned about buoyancy and density.]

_____

_____

Planets in the Great Beyond

Eris: discovered in 2005, Eris is slightly larger than Pluto and orbits three times as far from the sun as Pluto

exoplanets: planets that orbit stars other than the sun; also called *extrasolar planets*

luminous: emitting light

transit: the passage of a smaller astronomical object or its shadow across the luminous disk of a larger object

In their search for extraterrestrial life, astronomers look for planets within a star's habitable zone—the area where temperatures are perfect for liquid water to exist if water is present.

In 2007, two planets were discovered in or near the habitable zone of *Gliese 581*, a star 20.4 light years from Earth in the constellation of Libra. If evidence of water is found for either planet, they might be good candidates for supporting life.

How do scientists detect planets in other solar systems?

Although an undiscovered planet could exist beyond **Eris**, for now, astronomers agree that our solar system has eight planets and three dwarf planets. However, the stars in the night sky are distant suns burning away in their own corners of the universe. Do any of them have orbiting planets as well? The answer is a definite "Yes!" Astronomers have discovered well over 200 **exoplanets** so far.

The first scientific confirmation of planets beyond our solar system didn't occur until the 1990s, but the idea had been around for a long time. In 1713, Sir Isaac Newton had even argued that if our sun was a star and it had planets, it only made sense that other stars would too.

Detecting planets so far from Earth is a difficult task. Stars burn brightly enough to be seen across trillions of miles of space, but planets are about a million times less **luminous**. Besides, a star's brightness makes anything around it difficult see.

Telescopes aren't much use in locating dim, distant objects like exoplanets, so scientists use other, less-direct methods. The simplest is probably the **transit** method. When a large planet's orbit carries it in front of a star, the star's brightness is affected. Highly precise instruments can detect even the slightest change in a star's luminosity. If a star dims at regular intervals, it tells scientists that a planet might be circling it.

If a star's position in the sky appears to shift slightly side-to-side, this motion can also indicate the presence of an orbiting planet. Sometimes, as a smaller object orbits a larger object, gravity pulls the larger object around in a slight circular motion. For example, if you attach a heavy object to a string and then swing it around, you'll feel the weight pulling your hand around in a tight circle. From Earth, the star appears to move side to side.

Instruments can also detect infrared light around a star. Orbiting dust particles absorb the heat a star emits, and these instruments create images of the hot spots. Scientists then look closely for any indication of a large, solid object—most likely a planet.

Astronomers have begun researching the atmospheres and chemical compositions of these exoplanets. Now, the search has begun for Earth's twin.

Circle the letter of the best answer to the question below.

1. How many planets are there in the universe?

   a. 8

   b. 11

   c. about 200

   d. Scientists have no idea.

Write your answers on the lines below.

2. How might the transit method be used to determine an exoplanet's size and speed of orbit?

   _____

   _____

3. Star A emits twice as much heat and light as Star B. Is Star A's habitable zone nearer or farther away than Star B's? How do you know?

   _____

   _____

Unifying Concepts and Processes

Explain how states of matter play a role in why stars are visible across light years of space but planets are not. [Hint: How does the light emitted by stars and planets differ?]

_____

_____

_____

What's Next?

NASA is leading the way in the search for exoplanets, combining information from Earth-based telescopes with data collected by space-based instruments. Do some research to learn about the twin Keck telescopes or the Kepler mission. You can also learn how Earth's extremophiles help scientists research possible extraterrestrial life forms.

Living with the Stars

nebula: a cloud of interstellar gas and dust

protostar: a celestial object made of condensing interstellar material, mostly hydrogen gas

main sequence: the stable, middle stage of a star's life

red giant: the later stage of a dwarf star's life, when it has expanded and emits less energy

planetary nebula: outer layer of plasma emitted during the final stage of a star's life

white dwarf: extremely dense, bright, and hot remnant of a dying star

supernova: a sudden, powerful burst of electromagnetic energy emitted by a collapsing supergiant

neutron star: extremely dense mass of neutrons

About 10 percent of the stars in the Milky Way are white dwarf stars.

Betelgeuse—the upper left star in the constellation of Orion—is a red supergiant. Even without a telescope, you can see that it's slightly red in comparison to the surrounding stars.

Have the stars always been there, and will they last forever?

Step outside on a clear night, and you'll see the exact same stars, with a few exceptions, that human beings have been viewing since the dawn of civilization. Each little light might seem like a permanent fixture in space, but stars, like nearly everything else, exist for a while and then they don't.

A star's life begins in a massive cloud of dust particles, hydrogen gas, and plasma called a **nebula**. As gravity slowly pulls the individual pieces of matter together, the cloud becomes increasingly dense. Eventually, a **protostar** forms deep inside the cloud, and much of the gravitational energy that had been pulling everything together changes into heat energy. The temperature rises until it's high enough to trigger nuclear fusion, and the **main sequence** stage of the star's life begins.

A star spends nearly 90 percent of its existence in this stage, fusing hydrogen into helium and releasing heat and light. Our sun is a main sequence yellow dwarf star, but the universe is mostly filled with red dwarf stars that are about half our sun's size and don't emit as much energy.

After about ten billion years, dwarf stars run low on hydrogen, and the helium atoms begin fusing to form carbon. At the same time, these stars begin to swell and change into cooler **red giants**. The sun is no exception. It will eventually cool and expand beyond the orbits of Mercury and Venus— possibly even beyond Earth's orbit.

As the energy in a red giant slowly decreases, the outer materials begin drifting off to form a **planetary nebula**. All that remains in the end is a small, hot core called a **white dwarf**. Most white dwarfs are about the size of Earth, but they are incredibly dense. Astronomers estimate that more than 95 percent of all stars eventually become white dwarfs.

The universe's largest stars, called *supergiants*, are the exceptions. They form in the same way dwarf stars do, but supergiants last only millions—not billions—of years. They quickly use up their available energy in order to support their massive size. As a supergiant runs low on fuel, it reaches a point where it can no longer support its own mass. In less than a second, the star collapses in on itself and explodes as a **supernova**. If any of the core remains after this violent eruption, it might become a **neutron star**. The cores of the most massive stars—dozens of times more massive than the sun—will become black holes.

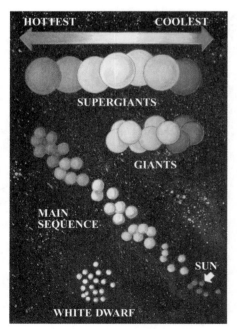

Circle the letter of the best answer to each question below.

1. What kind of star is our sun?

   a. a white dwarf

   b. a yellow dwarf

   c. a yellow giant

   d. a red giant

2. During a star's main sequence, it

   a. fuses hydrogen atoms to form helium.

   b. fuses helium atoms to form hydrogen.

   c. fuses hydrogen atoms to form carbon.

   d. fuses hydrogen with helium to create light.

3. Number the following stages of a star's life in the correct order.

   _____ Heat and light are emitted because of nuclear fusion.

   _____ Formation of a white dwarf.

   _____ Formation of a red giant.

   _____ Gas and dust inside a nebula are drawn together.

   _____ Planetary nebula drifts away.

Write your answer on the lines below.

4. How do you think the formation of new stars is related to supernovas and planetary nebulae?

   _____

   _____

Unifying Concepts and Processes

What does a star's color tell you about the amount of energy it emits?

   _____

What's Next?

Some of the Hubble Space Telescope's most amazing photographs have been of the Eagle Nebula, and the "Pillars of Creation" is one of the most famous images. Do some research to find them.

massive: containing a great quantity of matter

dense: containing matter that is closely packed together

space-time: a four-dimensional frame of reference—three dimensions of space and one of time

astrophysicists: scientists who study the physical and chemical processes of stars, galaxies, and space

infinitely: unlimited or immeasurable

The event horizon is the area in space where a black hole's gravity becomes strong enough to pull anything into it. Once something crosses the event horizon, there is no escape.

In 1974, physicist Stephen Hawking proved that black holes don't last forever. He discovered a tiny amount of radiation leaks from the event horizon. The largest black holes still last far longer than human beings can imagine, but eventually they run out of energy.

What happens inside a black hole?

Black holes may be the most mysterious objects in the universe. They are so **massive** and **dense** that they create an inescapable gravitational force. Anything that comes near enough will be sucked down inside the black hole where there is no escape. The gravity is so unimaginably powerful, it even captures light. This is how black holes get their name—they can't be seen because they don't emit or reflect electromagnetic energy.

In a previous chapter, you learned that gravity exists between masses. Photons are massless particles, though. How can light be affected by gravity? About 100 years ago, Albert Einstein gave us the answer.

Place several balls of different sizes on the ground, and then lay a striped sheet over them. Observe how the stripes become warped and curved wherever they cover a ball. Einstein's Theory of General Relativity explains that **space-time** is warped in a similar way around anything that has mass. The denser an object is, the more mass it has in a limited space and the more it will warp space-time. This warping is gravity. Although photons don't have any mass, light still moves through space-time. If you imagine the stripes are beams of light, then you can see how they also warp and bend around the objects with mass and density.

In the 1930s, **astrophysicists** began predicting the existence of black holes based on Einstein's work. They suspected that the most massive stars eventually collapsed into **infinitely** dense, singular points of matter. These "black holes" would be the densest, most massive objects in the universe. Light waves wouldn't just warp around them—they would be sucked inside, like water down a drain. Black holes can be as small as atoms or as large as several miles in width, but they are all infinitely dense.

Because all forms of matter and energy are pulled down into black holes, they can't be detected directly. Astronomers have to use other means instead. Throughout the universe, less massive objects orbit more massive objects, so scientists study the way stars move through space. A star that appears to be in orbit around an empty area is most likely circling a black hole. By measuring the star and its motion, astrophysicists can determine the size and mass of the black hole. They also look for areas in space that appear distorted, because a black hole will bend the light coming from more distant stars.

Circle the letter of the best answer to each question below.

1. An object that is pulled into a black hole will become

   a. more massive.

   b. denser.

   c. a plasma.

   d. Both a and b

2. Why is light affected by gravity?

   a. Because light consists of tiny particles of mass, called *photons*

   b. Because light waves bump up against objects that have mass

   c. Because light waves follow the curve of space-time

   d. Because light is denser than objects that have mass

Write your answers on the lines below.

3. Why are black holes invisible?

   _____

4. How can a black hole be massive but not big?

   _____

   _____

5. Why do stars orbit black holes and not the other way around?

   _____

   _____

6. Do you think black holes are hot, cold, or neither? Explain your answer.

   _____

   _____

What's Next?

Is Earth in danger of being pulled into a black hole? Why do scientists think supermassive black holes can be found at the centers of galaxies? Do black holes grow bigger over time? Do some research to find out.

Circle the letter of the best answer to each question below.

1. Geysers are located

   a. near areas of volcanic activity.

   b. only in Yellowstone National Park.

   c. only where magma mixes with water.

   d. All of the above

2. What makes metamorphic rock different from other types of rock?

   a. It has a glossy surface.

   b. It contains the remains of organisms.

   c. It's denser.

   d. It's a single color.

3. A star's energy, in the form of heat and light, is created by

   a. nebulas.

   b. oxidation.

   c. nuclear fission.

   d. nuclear fusion.

Write your answers on the lines below.

4. What role does interpretation play in meteorology?

   _____

5. Why do ice cores have visible layers?

   _____

6. What three conditions are necessary for a geyser to form?

   _____

7. What geological event cut channels into the landscape and created the upper Mississippi River?

   _____

8. Why does the Mediterranean region experience earthquakes and volcanic activity?

   _____

9. Explain the difference between igneous and sedimentary rocks.

_____

10. What is a star's habitable zone?

_____

11. Describe one way an astronomer might detect a planet orbiting a distant star.

_____

12. What force brings dust particles and gas together in order to form a star?

_____

13. Explain how black holes get their name.

_____

14. What happens to an object that crosses a black hole's event horizon?

_____

Use the words in the box to complete the sentences below.

magma	luminous	tectonic	glacial
sequence	estuary	persistence	

15. The _____ method of forecasting assumes that the weather won't change.

16. Ice core data indicates that eight _____ periods have occurred in the last 800,000 years.

17. Thousands of years ago, Cairo, Illinois, was a(n) _____ where the Mississippi River met the open sea.

18. Deep below Earth's surface, high temperatures change rock into _____.

19. The movement of Earth's _____ plates broke up Pangaea and created the Mediterranean Sea.

20. Exoplanets are difficult to see because the stars they orbit are a million times more

_____.

21. Stars spend most of their existence in the main _____ stage.

Lesson 5.1 Fighting Crime with Science

forensic science: the application of science to solve crimes

DNA fingerprint: also called *genetic fingerprint*; an individual's unique sequence of DNA base pairs

In 1892, Francis Galton proved that fingerprints are unique. That's why they can be reliably used to prove that a person was in a particular place or touched a certain object, like a doorknob or a weapon. Today, computer technology allows investigators to record the prints and quickly share them.

Teeth provide valuable information to forensic odontologists. Matching up a set of teeth to existing dental records can provide positive identification of a victim. Even bite marks found on a piece of chewing gum at a crime scene can provide evidence. A cast can be made of the teeth from their imprints on the gum. This cast can be compared with the teeth of a suspect and provide identification.

What role does science play in criminal investigations?

If you've ever watched one of the popular crime investigation shows on TV, you're probably familiar with **forensic science**—the application of science to solve crimes. The real-life practice of forensics isn't usually quite as dramatic as it appears on television. Still, it's an interesting profession that combines several different fields of science.

Without realizing it, we leave behind traces of ourselves wherever we go. It may be a can of soda or a crumpled piece of paper, or it could be hair, saliva, or tiny flakes of dry skin. Most of the time, these traces hold no real importance. If a crime has been committed, however, then these clues become evidence.

Using the expertise of scientists with different specialties can create a strong case, and it can assure the team that their conclusions are correct. A forensic anthropologist can gather clues by looking at bones or skeletons. The amount of wear can show how old a person was at the time of death. Bones can also be a source of information about a person's life and habits. For example, the bones of a runner would look different than those of a non-athlete. A chemical analysis can even reveal information about a person's diet. Forensic anthropologists can create a description of a person—including gender, height, weight, age, and ethnicity—based on a skeleton.

Forensic biologists analyze samples of hair, saliva, and blood. Each of these can be a source of a **DNA fingerprint**—a sample of a person's unique genetic code. The DNA of a crime suspect can be compared with DNA found at the scene of a crime to see if they match. Only identical twins share the same DNA, so DNA is considered a reliable source of evidence.

Analyzing handwriting can be a clue to a person's identity, but many people today use computers. New software allows investigators to match a printed page with the printer that produced it—a technique useful in locating people who make counterfeit money, fake passports, or other illegal documents. Even if writing or printing has been erased from a page, using ultraviolet light can allow investigators to see the missing words.

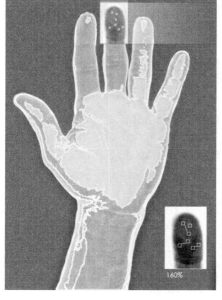

If you're interested in forensics, take as many science classes as you can. A background in medicine and criminology can also be helpful. If you're good at solving puzzles, forensics might be the field for you—evidence is only useful if someone can put the pieces together.

Write your answers on the lines below.

1. A burglar robbed the Larsons' house while they were on vacation. Once the burglar realized they were out of town, he wasn't in any hurry to finish the job. He had a snack, leaving the partially eaten leftovers on the counter. He watched part of a football game while leaning back and relaxing on the couch. He even took a shower and shaved before departing with many of the Larsons' valuables. What sorts of evidence could forensic investigators hope to collect at the Larsons' house? Give as many examples as you can.

   _____

   _____

   _____

2. How does a forensic anthropologist gather information?

   _____

3. Give two examples of the role that technology plays in forensics.

   _____

   _____

4. Forensic science is based on the idea that people leave _____.

5. One shortcoming of DNA fingerprinting is that only segments of DNA are used instead of the whole strand. The segment may not be completely unique, which makes it a less-reliable source of identification. In addition, human interpretation plays a role, and people can make mistakes. What is one way to ensure a mistake hasn't been made?

   _____

   _____

What's Next?

Try dusting for fingerprints yourself. Spread a bit of dust from a charcoal briquette over an area where you know there are fingerprints. Use a piece of clear packing tape to lift the fingerprints from the source. Apply the piece of tape to a sheet of white paper, and you should be able to see the prints.

Putting Nature to Work

transgenic technology: the process of transferring genes from one organism into an organism of a different species

biodegradable: able to be broken down into harmless products by microorganisms

bioremediation: the use of organisms to break down or remove toxic or contaminated materials from the environment

The Frozen Ark is a DNA bank that preserves the genetic material of animals around the world that are threatened with extinction. The DNA is frozen at a temperature of -80°C (-112°F). In the future, this frozen genetic material may be used to create clones of animals that have become extinct or disappeared in the wild. The Frozen Ark is an assurance that more of our planet's biodiversity won't be lost in coming years. The organization's goal is to collect the DNA and tissue of the 16,000 species on the World Conservation Union's Red List of threatened species.

What is biotechnology, and what role does it play in science today?

Biotechnology is the use of living organisms to create products, solve problems, or do tasks that benefit human beings. Some of the earliest examples were the use of yeast in fermentation and the crossbreeding of plants to produce species with desirable traits. Since that time, human abilities in the sciences have progressed and the technology has become more complex and advanced.

Today, scientists have the ability to use the smallest parts of organisms—their cells and molecules. For example, a geneticist can transfer the gene of one organism, like a fish, into a totally different species, like a plant, to give the plant a characteristic of the fish—such as hardiness in cold temperatures. This process is known as **transgenic technology**. The genes of an organism can also be altered to create desirable traits. The same results might be achieved over a longer period of time through selective breeding or even through evolution. Biotechnology can make the changes happen almost immediately.

Cloning animals is an example of biotechnology that is still fairly new and controversial. Someday, these cloned animals could be better able to resist disease and yield more meat or produce more milk. So far, however, they're actually less healthy than conventional animals. The concept of duplicating living creatures raises ethical issues, and opponents are also concerned about the future of cloning in the human population.

In addition to its uses in genetics, biotechnology also has many uses in the area of waste management. As the health of the planet becomes an important issue for us all, finding ways to be more environmentally friendly have also grown in importance. Biotechnology has been used to create **biodegradable** materials. One promising example is of a plastic-like material made through the fermentation of corn stalks. Unlike most plastics, it won't linger on Earth for thousands of years after it has been discarded.

Bioremediation involves using organisms to help clean up the environment. Many forms of bacteria already do this naturally. What excites scientists is the chance to create bacteria that could target specific environmental problems. For example, genetically modified bacteria could break down toxic or hazardous materials in landfills or after a chemical spill.

Use the words in the box to complete the sentences below.

fermentation	biodegradable	biodiversity	cloning

1. The Frozen Ark will help preserve some of Earth's amazing _____.

2. _____ is the use of biotechnology to create genetic copies of animals that have desirable characteristics.

3. Yogurt is an example of biotechnology because live cultures of bacteria added to milk cause

   _____ to take place.

4. A material that remains in its original form for thousands of years without breaking down is not

   considered _____.

Write your answers on the lines below.

5. Why is crossbreeding plants an example of biotechnology?

   _____

   _____

6. What is the Frozen Ark? What is its primary goal?

   _____

   _____

7. Explain what bioremediation is and how it is used.

   _____

   _____

8. Why isn't evolution of characteristics in an organism considered biotechnology?

   _____

What's Next?

Genetically modified foods are the product of plants whose genes were altered. Some people support the use of GM crops, while others are wary about eating the foods these crops produce. Unless a label states that a product contains no genetically modified ingredients, it probably does. Do some research to learn more about the pros and cons of this form of biotechnology. What are your views on it?

Magnets in Motion

commercial: suitable for the public and done with the goal of making money

maglev: shortened form of *magnetic levitation*

electromagnets: devices made from coils of wire wrapped around metal cores that become magnetized with the addition of electricity

Maglev trains need extremely powerful magnetic fields in order to suspend something as heavy as an entire train, so they use very heavy electromagnets. The additional weight makes the trains less efficient. Researchers are looking into superconductors as a solution. These special metals and alloys are extremely efficient conductors of electromagnetic forces when they are cooled to low temperatures.

Maglev train lines are being proposed to link Baltimore with Washington, D.C., and Los Angeles with Las Vegas.

Maglev trains don't use engines, so they don't pollute the air. They do use electricity, though, so some pollution might be created, depending on how the electricity was generated.

Is this cutting edge technology the future of transportation?

Since 2002, people in China have had the option of flying from downtown Shanghai to the city's outlying airport. They zoom along at average speeds approaching 200 miles per hour and complete the journey in less than eight minutes. They aren't flying in an airplane, though, and they certainly aren't soaring over anyone's head—in fact, they're barely half an inch above ground! The passengers are riding in the world's first high-speed, **commercial maglev** train.

A traditional train rolls along on slotted wheels that fit over a pair of metal rails. A massive engine at the front turns the wheels as it drags the long line of cars stretching behind it. A lot of energy is used up just overcoming friction—every one of the train's hundreds of wheels touches the tracks. Maglev trains are much more efficient. There's no friction because they hover above the track's surface as they move forward.

Although two different types of maglev technologies are being tested and put to use today, they both use electromagnetic forces to levitate the trains and propel them forward. One technology uses the repulsive action of like charges. Electrical currents are used to induce one magnetic field along the side of the train and another one along raised walls running down both sides of the track. These magnetic fields have the same charge, so they repel each other. The train is pushed upward slightly and suspended in the air. Separate **electromagnets** inside the surrounding walls are put to use pulling and pushing the train forward.

The Shanghai maglev train uses a different design. The train's body wraps around a steel rail running below it. Electromagnets in the lowest part of the train below the rail are attracted to an oppositely-charged magnetic field in the rail above. This attraction pulls the train upward just enough so that it no longer touches anything. Then, magnets in the surrounding walls propel the train forward.

Only a handful of maglev train systems are in the planning stages today, even though they are one of the most efficient means of transportation available. Part of the problem is that the initial costs of building them are extremely high. They can't use existing train tracks, so the entire system has to be built from scratch. Once a maglev train is up and running, though, it can't be beat for speed and efficiency.

Circle the letter of the best answer to each question below.

1. Maglev train systems aren't common around the world yet because

    a. electromagnetic technology isn't widely understood.

    b. electromagnets are extremely difficult to create.

    c. they are still very expensive to develop.

    d. All of the above

2. Which of the following statements about maglev trains is true?

    a. The first car of the train contains an engine.

    b. The train is pushed along by power supplied only to the last car.

    c. The entire train is propelled forward as a single unit.

    d. The train moves because it is made of metal that is attracted to magnets in the track.

Write your answers on the lines below.

3. List two reason why maglev trains are highly efficient.

    _____

4. Do the cars of a maglev train need to be connected to each other? Why or why not?

    _____

    _____

5. At low speeds, maglev trains are nearly silent, but at their top speeds, they can be very loud. Why do you think the amount of noise the train makes depends on how quickly it travels?

    _____

    _____

Unifying Concepts and Processes

Once a maglev train is moving, do you think the amount of electromagnetic force has to increase when the train goes up a hill? Explain your answer.

_____

_____

Welcome to the Digital Revolution

binary: having two parts

pixels: the smallest units of an image produced on a monitor or printer; the word *pixel* is short for "picture element"

analog: representing information by using one or more physical properties that are expressed along a continuous scale

signals: changing quantities that can be used to represent information; for example, fluctuating electrical currents, radio waves, lights, or sounds can be controlled to become signals carrying information

Computer software contains digital information that tells a computer's hardware how and when to perform specific functions.

Because it's broken up into thousands of distinct pieces, digital information is easier to manipulate.

In a binary number system, only the digits 0 and 1 are used. Here's an example of how your computer counts from 0 to 9:

0
1
10
11
100
101
110
111
1000
1001

What does it mean to say that something is digital?

Digital music, digital television, digital cameras, and digital phones. In the last 20 years, the gadgets we use to process and convey information have almost all incorporated digital technology. But what does that mean, exactly? Although the word *digital* is used to describe many modern electronic products, most people aren't exactly sure how they are different from electronic products used in the past.

Your first guess might be that digital technology has something to do with computers. In a way, that's correct, because computers store information in digital code, and digital code is at the heart of all digital technology.

Digital code is way of representing any kind of information—a sound, an image, a text—as a series of numbers. Most digital electronics, including computers, use **binary** code that consists of strings of 1s and 0s. This code is created and passed along with rapid pulses of electricity, like Morse code. When a current is on, it equals 1, and when it's off, it equals 0.

In order for information to become digital, it first has to be broken down into many smaller, distinct pieces. Each piece is then assigned a unique binary number. When the pieces are reassembled, they allow the original information to be understood again. For example, if you enlarge a digital image on a computer screen, you can see the individual **pixels** of information that work together to create the image. The color of each pixel was determined by a unique sequence of 1s and 0s.

Before the digital age, information was created, stored, sent, and received as **analog signals**. Analog technologies don't break information down into separate, distinct pieces. If you enlarge a traditional photograph, you won't see a distinct grid of pixels like you do in digital photos. Instead, the colors blend into each other smoothly. In music, an analog recording captures the entire sound wave generated by a singer or instrument. A digital recording breaks the sound wave up into pieces that can be assigned digital codes.

With the right equipment, any piece of information can be broken down and translated into a series of electronic pulses. Video monitors, cell phones, and CD players, along with so many other digital gadgets in our lives, read the electronic codes and change the information back into sounds, images, and other forms we can readily understand.

Circle the letter of the best answer to each question below.

1. Computers are digital technologies because they

    a. are electronic.

    b. store and use numerically coded information.

    c. process information.

    d. All of the above

2. When you print an image that was taken from a computer, the photograph contains

    a. visual information.

    b. digital code.

    c. binary colors.

    d. All of the above

Write your answers on the lines below.

3. Is the way you experience sights and sounds in the world around you more similar to digital information or analog information? Why?

    _____

    _____

4. Do you think a binary code can be transmitted by light, sound, or radio waves, or only by using an electrical current? Explain your answer.

    _____

    _____

What's Next?

Binary numbers might appear confusing, but they aren't as different from decimal numbers as you might think. In the number 1,568, the first number represents 1 X 1000, the second number 5 X 100, the third number 6 X 10, and the last number 8 X 1. Instead of representing powers of ten, each digit in a binary number represents powers of two. From right to left, the spaces represent 1, 2, 4, 8, 16, 32, and so on. This means that the binary number 111101 equals the decimal number 61. Break it down and you get (1 X 1) + (0 X 2) + (1 X 4) + (1 X 8) + (1 X 16) + (1 X 32) for a total of 61. What are the decimal equivalents of 101010 or 1000111? Can you write 45 as a binary number?

versatile: capable of performing many different tasks

amplify: make larger or more powerful

switch: an electronic device used for making, breaking, or changing connections in an electrical circuit

transistor: an electronic device that controls electric currents, usually acting as an amplifier or switch

vacuum tubes: sealed glass tubes with the air removed, in which electrons move from a negatively charged conductor, called a *cathode*, to a positively charged anode

In 1956, William Shockley, John Bardeen, and Walter Brattain—scientists from Bell Labs—won the Nobel Prize in physics for their research.

Ever since the integrated circuit, or microchip, was first developed in 1959, its size has continually shrunk through the years. Engineers today are preparing for a new generation of microchips that will be so small, they may have to be assembled one molecule at a time.

What do transistors have to do with microchips?

In 1948, scientists at Bell Labs unveiled a new invention to the world. This tiny, **versatile** device could quickly and precisely **amplify** electrical currents. It could also act as a **switch**, sending currents in whichever direction was necessary. At the time, few people took notice of this new technology, but today it's inside every computer, cell phone, and television. The **transistor** revolutionized the world of electronics.

For nearly 40 years, from 1920 to 1960, most electronic devices used **vacuum tubes** to control the flow of electricity inside them. Vacuum tubes are similar to incandescent light bulbs—they contain filaments inside sealed glass tubes. They also create a lot of heat and eventually burn out like light bulbs. Transistors perform the same function, but they're incredibly small, inexpensive, and don't generate as much heat. Transistors can also be made in a much wider range of sizes, so they can control even the tiniest currents. Even better, they seldom burn out the way vacuum tubes do.

Transistors are made of substances called *semiconductors*, the most common of which is silicon. Semiconductors have crystal structures, and their atoms are arranged in a way that keeps electrons from moving easily from atom to atom. In other words, they act like insulators. However, if another substance is mixed in and becomes part of the crystal structure, the material becomes a conductor. It's this ability to control whether the material will act as a conductor or an insulator that makes semiconductors so useful.

The first American transistors were mainly manufactured for and sold to the military. However, a Japanese company decided to use transistors to create tiny, portable radios. Most portable radios in the mid-50s still used vacuum tubes, so they were bulky and heavy. By the early 1960s, America was flooded with small, inexpensive transistor radios from Japan. The transistors amplified the signals received by the antenna and broadcast them from a tiny speaker on the radio's side. Compared to the sound quality people are used to today, transistor radios sounded tinny and small.

Transistors allowed the miniaturization and portability of many other electronic products. When the microchip was invented in 1959, it greatly increased the power and efficiency of transistors by placing several of them onto a slice of semiconductor. Today, a single microchip can contain billions of tiny transistors organizing the electrical currents of our digital world.

Circle the letter of the best answer to each question below.

1. Which of the following statements is correct?

   a. Semiconductors are made of transistors.

   b. Microchips contain many individual transistors.

   c. Transistors are made of microchips.

   d. A single transistor might contain thousands of microchips.

2. The most commonly used semiconductor is

   a. the transistor.

   b. the integrated circuit.

   c. silicon.

   d. copper wire.

Write your answers on the lines below.

3. List three advantages transistors have over vacuum tubes.

   _____

   _____

4. Why are semiconductors such useful substances for electrical systems?

   _____

5. Explain how transistors allowed for the miniaturization and portability of electronic devices.

   _____

   _____

Unifying Concepts and Processes

A vacuum tube controls the flow of electrons that pass through it. In order to create a vacuum, nearly all of the air must be removed from the tube. What advantage do you think is gained by removing air from the space in which electrons will be traveling?

   _____

   _____

Explosive Power

cylinder: the hollow, cylindrical chamber in which pressure from an ignited gas or liquid moves a sliding piston

pistons: solid cylinders or disks that fit inside hollow cylinders and slide back and forth

gears: wheels with teeth around their rims that fit between the teeth of other gears

alternator: an electric generator that creates AC electricity

Jets and rockets also use internal combustion engines, but the ignited fuel isn't contained inside a cylinder the way it is in a car motor. Instead, the explosion is allowed to shoot out of an opening in the back of the engine. Because of Newton's third law of motion, the vehicle is propelled forward as a reaction to the exhaust shooting in the opposite direction.

How does an internal combustion engine change fuel into work?

From lawnmowers, tractors, and automobiles, to ships, jets, and rockets, the moving machines of our world are almost all powered by combustion. With just a few exceptions, engines work because an explosive mixture of air, fuel, and fire gets the parts in motion.

An internal combustion engine—the most common engine in the world—traps air and fuel inside a small chamber, called a **cylinder**, and then adds a spark to ignite the mixture. The chemicals combust and quickly transform into hot, expanding gases. This creates tremendous pressure inside the chamber, which is used to move parts inside the engine.

The most common internal combustion engines—like the ones inside most cars—use the explosive pressure inside the cylinder to move a series of **pistons**. Like little seesaws, the pistons are paired up so that when one is forced downward by combustion, its partner is pushed back up.

The first downward motion of Piston 1 pulls fuel and air into its cylinder. When Piston 2 is forced downward by combustion in its own cylinder, Piston 1 goes back up and compresses the fuel mixture. Then, a spark ignites the mixture, and Piston 1 is driven back down again. When Piston 1 goes up the second time, it pushes the burnt gases out of the cylinder, and the cycle is ready to begin again. This is how a four-stroke engine works in most cars and trucks.

The movement of the pistons is used to spin several different **gears**, which are connected to belts and other gears that turn the cars' wheels, cool the engine, pump water and oil, and perform all the other important jobs that keep a car running. The beauty of internal combustion engines is that once they've been started, they should keep running as long as they have enough fuel. An engine can even generate its own electricity.

The initial spark that's needed to start an engine normally comes from a battery. Once the engine is running, though, the pistons spin gears that are attached to the car's **alternator**. Inside the alternator, a magnet spins at incredible speed. It's surrounded by a coil of wire, so the spinning magnetic field causes a current to flow through the wire, and the engine supplies its own electricity. This electricity provides the sparks necessary for combustion in the chambers, and it recharges the battery. Without an alternator, a car would need a new battery after every trip.

INDUCTION   COMPRESSION   POWER   EXHAUST

Circle the letter of the best answer to each question below.

1. In a four-stroke engine, as a piston moves up and down inside a cylinder, combustion occurs

   a. every time the piston moves upward.

   b. every time the piston moves downward.

   c. every other time the piston moves upward.

   d. every time the piston moves up or down.

2. The movement of the pistons

   a. draws fuel and air into the cylinder.

   b. pushes exhaust out of the cylinder.

   c. compresses the fuel and air in the cylinder.

   d. All of the above

Write your answers on the lines below.

3. Why does a car engine still need a battery if it can generate its own electricity?

   _____

4. How is a jet engine different from the engine that powers a car?

   _____

   _____

Unifying Concepts and Processes

1. Does a car's alternator use induction or conduction to create electricity?

   _____

2. Review the definitions of potential and kinetic energy. Then, use the two terms to describe what happens inside the cylinder of a working engine.

   _____

   _____

   _____

   _____

optical illusions: differences in what the brain perceives to be true and what is actually true about a visual stimulus

pigment: a chemical substance that determines color

Human beings have learned about camouflage by observing nature and use these lessons especially in hunting and warfare. Camouflage clothing employs color and pattern to conceal the wearer. Shades of green, brown, or tan are chosen to blend with the colors of the environment. Visually disruptive patterns are often used to hide the outline of the body and appear to the viewer to be a part of the surroundings.

How does camouflage work?

One of the most common survival adaptations in nature is camouflage. This ability to hide from predator or prey is accomplished by blending into the environment using color and texture. Camouflage develops over time through natural selection. Remember the gypsy moths in London during the Industrial Revolution? Though both light- and dark-wing moths existed, the species evolved so that eventually most of the moths had darker-colored wings. This allowed them to better blend in with the bark of trees that had darkened from air pollution. Animals that are able to remain undetected survive longer and go on to produce offspring that also carry the physical traits necessary for disguising themselves.

Camouflage relies on **optical illusions**. When an animal blends into its surroundings, an observer's eye cannot distinguish the shape of the animal in order to communicate to the brain that something is there. An animal's camouflage is designed to fool its predators, but it may not always deceive human beings. For example, the bold, black-and-white pattern of zebra fur does not blend in with the grasslands zebras inhabit. However, lions are colorblind, and zebras travel in herds. Stripes make it harder for a lion to distinguish the individual zebras within the herd.

A similar result is achieved by fish that are countershaded. When an attack comes from above, the dark upper body is more difficult for the predator to see against the water. A predator from below would encounter the light underbelly that is obscured by the bright surface of the water.

Some birds and mammals change color seasonally. The arctic fox has a dark coat in the spring and summer to better blend in with the ground. To prepare for winter, it molts, and grows a new white coat to match the snow-covered ground. Other animals, like reptiles, amphibians, and fish, can alter their skin color. They have deeper-level **pigment** cells called *chromatophores*. Certain cuttlefish species can manipulate their chromatophores by controlling muscles that surround each one. The constricting muscles squeeze the pigment to the top so that it becomes visible. These cuttlefish can generate many colors and patterns to blend in with various surroundings. Chameleons are the most famous color-changers, but their ability is a reflex response to their mood and the time of day.

Write **true** or **false** next to each statement below.

1. _____ Human beings used camouflage as a means of protection long before animals ever did.

2. _____ The appearance of some animals varies by season so that they can blend into their changing surroundings.

3. _____ Color, texture, and shape can all play a role in camouflage.

4. _____ Molting allows an animal to change color when a predator is near.

5. _____ An animal that is countershaded may be different colors, depending on the side from which it is viewed.

Write your answers on the lines below.

6. Explain how camouflage can be used by both predator and prey.

   _____

   _____

7. How do optical illusions work?

   _____

8. What role does natural selection play in the development of camouflage?

   _____

9. Human camouflage often includes the use of a visually disruptive pattern to confuse the viewer. Give an example not mentioned in the selection of an animal whose skin or fur contains a visually

   disrupting pattern. _____

10. What purpose do chromatophores serve?

   _____

11. What uses does camouflage have for human beings?

   _____

12. How does a zebra's camouflage fool its predator?

   _____

Tuning in to TV's Early Years

photoconductivity: the increase in a substance's electrical conductivity due to the absorption of light

mechanical: operated or produced by forces of motion, as opposed to chemical, electromagnetic, or nuclear forces

cathode ray tube: a special vacuum tube that generates a focused beam of electrons onto a fluorescent screen

The first successful color television system was developed in 1940 by Peter Goldmark. Once again, a spinning disk was put to use, this time with red, green, and blue sections that scanned a color image.

Cable TV began in 1948 when John Walson put an antenna on a mountaintop and ran cables to nearby homes that weren't getting good reception.

The Image Dissector needed extremely bright images to work, though—too bright to be practical. A more efficient device, based partly on Farnsworth's invention, was developed by Vladimir Zworykin. His CRT was a major component in the first TVs sold to the public.

What discoveries led to the invention of the television?

It's impossible to credit just a single person for the development of television. Scientists had been experimenting with ways of transmitting images for nearly 60 years before TVs hit the market in the early 1930s. Since then, TV technology has improved rapidly, and today we have plasma screens, HDTV, and movies on cell phones.

In 1873, electrical engineers Willoughby Smith and Joseph May discovered **photoconductivity**. While working with the element *selenium*, they noticed that its conductivity increased when it was hit with a bright light. This characteristic could be used to convert light waves into electrical pulses. In other words, patterns of light could be changed into electrical signals. That's still the most basic description of how televisions work.

The next big step was finding a way to transmit pictures using this new discovery. In 1884, German inventor Paul Nipkow devised the Nipkow disk. The spinning disk was placed in front of an illuminated image, and as light passed through tiny holes in the disk, the image was sliced into horizontal patterns of light. A lens then focused the patterns onto a layer of selenium cells. The light waves became electrical signals that moved through a wire, and at the other end, the electricity was used to reproduce the original image.

Other inventors improved Nipkow's scanning disk, and by the early 20th century, it was commonly used to transmit photographs through telephone lines. The photoconductors of the time couldn't react quickly enough, though, to capture the changing patterns in a moving image. In 1925, John Baird finally developed a **mechanical** scanning disk system that could do this, and the world's first moving televised images were broadcast.

Meanwhile, several other inventors had been working with the newly-invented **cathode ray tube**, or CRT. They were hoping that CRTs would lead to an electrical scanning method that didn't rely on a spinning, mechanical disk. In 1927, 20-year-old farmer Philo Farnsworth unveiled his breakthrough technology—a special CRT called an *Image Dissector*. It focused an image onto a photoconducting material, which then emitted electrons in a pattern that echoed the image. The electron "image" was then used to create electrical signals. It was the first completely electronic television system.

Circle the letter of the best answer to each question below.

1. What do all television systems have in common?

   a. They send and receive images by transmitting signals through the air.

   b. They convert images into electrical signals.

   c. They use CRTs to produce their images.

   d. All of the above

2. CRT stands for

   a. cable reception and transmission.

   b. cathode rasterization television.

   c. cathode ray tube.

   d. cathode reception television.

3. Telephone lines were used to transmit images that had been scanned by a Nipkow disk. This information tells you that telephone lines

   a. are photoconductors.

   b. carry electrical currents.

   c. use CRTs.

   d. are mechanical devices.

Write your answer on the line below.

4. How did the television system developed by Philo Farnsworth differ from the systems that came before?

   _____

Unifying Concepts and Processes

Many televisions can receive signals through antennas. Once an image has been converted into electrical signals, what additional step is necessary before they can be transmitted to a wireless TV?

_____

Living and Working in Space

microgravity: a condition in which there is so little gravity that weightlessness occurs

atrophy: the shrinking or wasting away of a body part or tissue

The ISS flies at a speed of about 17,000 miles per hour and orbits Earth once every 92 minutes. Looking out a window, its residents can view a sunrise or sunset every 45 minutes.

ISS is about the size of a football field and will be large enough for seven permanent residents.

The ISS was completed in 2010 and may be operational until 2028.

How was the International Space Station constructed, and what is its purpose?

Human beings have always dreamed about one day living in space. A lucky few astronauts and engineers have had the opportunity to live out this dream at the *International Space Station* (ISS). Once the Cold War ended, the United States and Russia decided to combine efforts and create the ISS. Both countries had been working on smaller stations, but by working together, a larger, more complex station could be built. They were soon joined by Japan, Canada, Brazil, and the countries of the European Space Agency.

It would be impossible to build the space station on the ground and then launch it into space. No rocket would be powerful enough. Instead, the most practical solution was to build it piecemeal in space. The first launch occurred in November of 1998. A Russian Proton rocket launched a control module called *Zarya* into space. It would provide the power and be a docking port for *Zvezda*—the living quarters that arrived in 2000. Several weeks later, *Zarya* was joined by the U.S. module, *Unity*. *Unity's* purpose was to link structures of the ISS together and to serve as a docking port. A few days after its arrival, the two modules were connected.

With the arrival of *Zvezda*, the space station could hold its first occupants. The module was 43-feet long and provided the basics of what a crew would need—a life support system to supply food and water and get rid of waste materials, and a source of electrical power. Later in the year, six 108-foot solar panels arrived that would provide power to the entire station using only the energy of the sun.

Over the next seven years, a variety of new components were added. Among the most important were several modules that would be used for scientific investigation. One of the purposes of the ISS is for scientists to have a place in which to carry out experimentation in various scientific fields. If human beings are ever going to spend long periods of time in space, it's important to learn what the long-term effects of **microgravity** are on the human body. We already know that it causes muscles and bones to **atrophy**, which is one reason that residents of the ISS exercise for about two hours a day. In addition to biological studies, physics, chemistry, astronomy, and meteorology are also topics of research. The station's environment of zero gravity, as well as its location approximately 220 miles above Earth, make it an ideal place for studies that can't be done on Earth.

Circle the letter of the best answer to each question below.

1. Why is exercise an important element of the day for residents of the space station?

   a. because they need to be in good shape for heavy lifting in space

   b. because they are often bored

   c. because bones and muscles atrophy more quickly in space

   d. because it's easier to gain weight in space than it is on Earth

2. Which of the following statements is not true?

   a. The space station orbits approximately 220 miles above Earth.

   b. The space station was finished in 2010.

   c. There have not yet been any residents at the space station.

   d. The ISS circles Earth about once every hour and a half.

Write your answers on the lines below.

3. Why is it practical for the ISS to be a collaborative effort between many of the world's countries?

   _____

4. Why does the space station have to be constructed in pieces?

   _____

5. What is the purpose of *Zvezda*?

   _____

6. What sorts of scientific investigations are done at the ISS? What condition makes the space station an interesting location for experimentation to take place?

   _____

   _____

What's Next?

As of April 2014, there have been 39 expeditions to the space station. Visit the NASA web site to learn more about each expedition and its crew, as well as planned missions.

Circle the letter of the best answer to each question below.

1. Bioremidation is used

   a. to clone animals.

   b. to transfer the genes of one organism into an organism of a different species.

   c. to remove or break down harmful substances in the environment.

   d. in crossbreeding to produce plants or animals with desirable traits.

2. What is a microchip?

   a. a collection of transistors

   b. a small vacuum tube

   c. a radio receiver

   d. All of the above

3. The International Space Station

   a. is a collaborative effort of many nations.

   b. will not be complete until 2016.

   c. is used to conduct scientific experiments in space.

   d. Both a and c

4. What causes a maglev train to levitate?

   a. two magnetic fields with like charges

   b. two magnetic fields with opposite charges

   c. strong air currents

   d. Either a or b

Write your answers on the lines below.

5. Give one example of a forensic scientist, and explain what he or she does.

   _____

   _____

6. What role does DNA play in forensics?

   _____

7. What is the purpose of the Frozen Ark?

   _____

8. Why are maglev trains much more efficient than many other transportation methods?

   _____

9. What has to happen to a piece of information in order for it to be translated into digital code?

   _____

10. Why did transistors quickly replace vacuum tubes in most electrical devices?

    _____

11. Explain what role optical illusions play in camouflage.

    _____

    _____

12. What is a photoconductor?

    _____

13. Explain how the International Space Station was constructed.

    _____

    _____

Underline the correct answer from the two choices you are given.

14. Biotechnology plays an important role in the creation of (biodegradable, transgenic) materials that are less damaging to the environment.

15. Maglev trains use (electromagnetic, gravitational) forces to float above their tracks.

16. Computers analyze digital information written as a (electronic, binary) number system.

17. Silicon is the most common (insulator, semiconductor) used in electronic devices.

18. A car engine's alternator (induces, conduces) an electrical current that can be used for combustion.

19. A (piston, gear) moves up and down inside each cylinder of an internal combustion engine.

20. Philo Farnsworth invented the first all (mechanical, electrical) television system.

Lesson 6.1 Stressed Out

insomnia: difficulty sleeping

endorphins: chemicals produced by the body that are natural painkillers and create a feeling of well-being

There are lots of effective ways of dealing with stress. Here are a few examples:

- Talking to a parent or friend can help you remember that someone cares and you aren't alone.

- Deep breathing (in for a count of four, hold for a count of two, and out for a count of four) can help you relax.

- Exercising—whether it's going for a walk, playing basketball, or dancing—produces **endorphins** which can counteract feelings of stress.

- Spending time doing something you enjoy, like reading, listening to music, playing with a pet, or cooking, can take your mind off your troubles.

- Relaxation exercises offer quick results. Just contract and then release each muscle in your body, starting at your toes and working your way up to your head.

How do you handle the stresses in your life?

Everyone experiences stress. It's a basic human reaction to situations that make us feel fear or anxiety. Stress evokes a response known as "fight or flight"—an instinctual reaction to these feelings. When confronted with a predatory animal, for example, our early ancestors had to make a snap decision to fight to defend themselves or to flee to safety. The physical symptoms that are often linked to stress are actually the result of blood being redirected from its normal path towards the body's large muscles and more vital organs—a reaction that prepares the body to take action. Feelings of stress and worry served a purpose in the early days of human history, and they continue to do so today.

While most people view stress as something negative, there are positive aspects to it. Feeling a little stressed about a presentation you have to give can make you work harder and prepare better. More often, though, stress has a negative impact on our lives. It can make it difficult to learn and remember things, cause depression, and change relationships. Stress can even lead to serious health problems like high blood pressure and heart attacks. Studies have also linked stress to unhealthy eating habits, particularly of fatty foods. If a habit like this persists over time, it can lead to obesity, which is associated with higher risks of diseases like cancer and diabetes.

Recognizing the signs and symptoms of stress in yourself are important. The way people handle stress varies. Your sister may seem extra crabby when she's stressed, while a friend may withdraw and act depressed. Other common signs of stress are an increased heart rate, headaches, **insomnia**, stomachaches, grinding or clenching teeth, loss of appetite, tense muscles in the shoulders and neck, dizziness, and a dry mouth.

The causes of stress are endless, and like the symptoms, they vary from person to person. For adolescents, common worries are often school, relationships with friends and family, sports, and issues related to home life—like money, moving, or the health of a family member. Feeling as though these issues are outside of your control makes the feelings of anxiety more intense. That's why it's so important to remember that even when you can't control the situation, you can control how you react to it.

Circle the letter of the best answer to the question below.

1. Which of the following is not usually associated with high levels of stress?

   a. headaches

   b. insomnia

   c. feelings of contentment and well-being

   d. overeating or loss of appetite

Write your answers on the lines below.

2. Identify and list three sources of stress in your life.

   _____

3. Explain the "fight or flight" response.

   _____

   _____

4. Give an example of a time you experienced stress and explain how you handled it. Do you think it was an effective method?

   _____

   _____

5. What are three things in your life that you can do to reduce stress?

   _____

   _____

6. Why is exercise a good source of relieving stress?

   _____

7. In what ways can stress have a positive impact on your life?

   _____

8. Reread the last line of the selection. Then, give an example that illustrates it.

   _____

   _____

Eating for Energy

cumulative: increasing through additions; formed by accumulation

glycogen: the form in which glucose (sugar) is stored in tissue, especially muscle

electrolytes: ions, like sodium and potassium, that regulate processes in the body and help cells communicate

Remember to drink lots of water before, during, and after exercising. The water you lose by sweating can cause your body to quickly become dehydrated. This is a serious condition that can lead to fatigue and heatstroke. In extreme circumstances, it can even lead to death. Drinking 6 to 8 ounces of cool water every 20 minutes or so while you exercise will keep your body hydrated. If you exercise for extended periods of time, you may want to try a sports drink that has sugars and **electrolytes**, which your body loses through sweat.

Can the foods you eat help improve your athletic performance?

You've been training hard, and you want to be at peak performance for the softball championships. You've heard about foods, drinks, and supplements that can boost your performance, but you're not sure if they work. Do you know what you should eat to be at your best?

Good nutrition is as important to your body as all the training and practicing you do. The effects of good nutrition are **cumulative**, though, so eating well just before a competition isn't enough to keep your body healthy. The best way to consistently get the nutrition you need is by eating a balanced diet. Different foods offer different benefits to your body, which is why variety is so important.

To find out what foods you should eat and how many servings a day are recommended for someone your size, you can visit www.mypyramid.gov. If you are an athlete or you have periods of high activity, you may need to eat more than the suggested number of servings. The more calories you burn, the more you need to eat to replenish your energy levels.

Some athletes believe they need high-protein diets or supplements to build muscles. It's true that an athlete needs more protein because both muscle building and aerobic exercise can burn protein for energy. However, it's easy to add protein to your diet by eating extra fish, lean meats, beans, eggs, and nuts. Fresh, whole foods are the best source of nutrition.

Another popular practice for endurance athletes is called *carbo-loading*. An athlete eats few carbohydrates (like bread, pasta, and cereal) but lots of fats and proteins in the days before a competition. A day or two before the event, he or she eats lots of carbs to replenish the body's stores of **glycogen**. This practice can put unnecessary stress on the body. The better solution is to simply boost the amount of carbs you eat before a competition and reduce your workout time so that you have a good supply of glycogen ready when you need it.

The best way to prepare your body for an athletic event is to eat a meal that's easy to digest three hours beforehand. Fats are hard to digest and sugary foods can cause your blood-sugar to soar and then plummet. Your best bet is a light meal that is high in starches—especially complex carbohydrates, like whole grains—and has a little protein. It'll fill you up and give you the energy you need to do your best.

MyPyramid.gov
STEPS TO A HEALTHIER YOU

Write **true** or **false** next to each statement below.

1. _____ In general, athletes and non-athletes should consume the same number of calories per day.

2. _____ Fatigue and poor performance are the only effects of dehydration.

3. _____ It's important to drink water before, during, and after exercising.

4. _____ It is a myth that athletes need extra protein in their diets.

Use the words in the box to complete the sentences below.

glycogen	supplements	protein	hydrated

5. Drinking a glass of water about three times an hour during exercise will keep your body

_____.

6. Fresh, whole foods are a better source of nutrition than _____.

7. Salmon, walnuts, and black beans are all good sources of _____.

8. A good supply of _____ can give your body the extra energy it needs to perform well.

Write your answers on the lines below.

9. Why is eating a variety of foods an important part of a nutritious diet?

_____

10. What benefits are there to having a sports drink that contains electrolytes when you're exercising for a long period of time?

_____

11. Give an example of a good meal to have before a sporting event and explain why.

_____

_____

12. In general, complex carbs are a better choice than simple carbs because they take longer to digest. Explain why you think this makes them a more healthful choice.

_____

Good Enough to Eat

additives: small amounts of substances that change the properties of the material to which they're added

food-borne illnesses: illnesses caused by eating foods that contain bacteria, viruses, or toxins

Food, drugs, and cosmetics aren't the only products regulated by the FDA. Medical devices (like pacemakers), biologics (like vaccines), and radiation-emitting products (like microwaves) are also the agency's responsibility.

The FDA monitors foods that are imported from foreign countries to make sure they meet U.S. standards of safety. Even so, this can be difficult to do. In 2007, a massive pet food recall occurred. Manufacturing plants in China had included a substance called *melamine* as filler in pet foods. It isn't approved for use in food, but the plants didn't disclose that they were using it. It wasn't until animals began getting sick, and even dying, that the tainted food was traced to China.

How do you know that the food you eat each day is safe to consume?

For breakfast, you have some cereal, milk, fruit, and juice. Then, you open up a bottle of water and take your antibiotics for a sore throat you had last week. As you're leaving for school, you grab some lip balm and smear it on. You may not realize it, but the United States government was responsible for making sure that each of those products you used was safe. More specifically, it was the responsibility of the FDA, an agency of the U.S. Department of Health and Human Services.

The FDA was created in 1906 when President Theodore Roosevelt signed the Food and Drugs Act into law. The purpose of the agency was to ensure that food wasn't spoiled and didn't contain fillers that compromised its quality, coloring that hid any problems with it, or **additives** that could be harmful. Similar criteria were applied to pharmaceutical drugs. The law also said that manufacturers had to be truthful about what their products contained and couldn't misrepresent any benefits.

In 1938, the Food, Drug, and Cosmetics Act was signed into law by President Franklin Roosevelt. It included stricter regulations and gave the FDA more authority. More than 100 people had died after taking a drug that wasn't properly tested. It was now the job of the FDA to ensure the safety of such products by doing further testing. Factory inspection became a part of the agency's duties, as did monitoring the safety of cosmetics.

Today, the food supply in the U.S. is one of the safest in the world. All aspects of the food industry are examined to make sure they adhere to safe practices and that their products are free of contamination. This includes any places where food is manufactured or packaged. It also includes places where food is served, like grocery stores, restaurants, and schools.

Part of the job of the FDA is to conduct research on food safety issues and educate the public about safe food practices. There are more than 75 million cases of **food-borne illnesses** that occur every year. Many of these cases could be prevented through proper handling, storage, and preparation of foods. The more people who are knowledgeable about safe food practices, the fewer illnesses and deaths will occur.

When a problem with a product does arise, it is the responsibility of the FDA to issue a recall. It informs consumers that there is a safety problem and advises them to stop using the product.

Write your answers on the lines below.

1. Why was the FDA created?

   _____

   _____

2. What is a recall? What causes one to occur?

   _____

   _____

3. Why is educating the public an important role of the FDA? Be specific.

   _____

   _____

4. An emulsifier causes water and oil to stay mixed together instead of separating in products like

   mayonnaise and ice cream. It is an example of _____.

5. Give examples of three non-food products that are the responsibility of the FDA.

   _____

6. The 2007 pet food recall occurred because manufacturing plants in China weren't disclosing all the substances they were using. Do you think the FDA could have done more to prevent something like this from happening? If so, how?

   _____

   _____

7. Not only does the FDA monitor foods intended for human beings, it also regulates animal feed and drugs. This is done partly for the safety of the animals, and partly for the safety of human beings. Explain how human beings might be affected by the foods animals consume.

   _____

   _____

What's Next?

The FDA is not responsible for all food products. Do some research to find out what foods are the responsibility of the USDA and why.

UVA and UVB rays: waves of electromagnetic radiation produced by the sun

synthetic: artificial; human-made

polymers: long, chainlike molecules found in organic substances like protein and wood; also used in the creation of synthetic materials, like plastics and fibers

For people working or traveling in extremely cold conditions, having the proper protective clothing is essential. The layer closest to the body wicks away moisture due to perspiration. The next layer must provide insulation to keep the body's heat from escaping. Polar fleece is a popular material for this layer because it is warm and dries quickly. The outer layer must be hydrophobic (which literally means "scared of water") and able to resist strong winds. A popular choice for this layer is a synthetic material that lets water vapor escape without allowing any moisture to penetrate it.

How many purposes does your clothing serve?

Most people regard clothing simply as a form of covering for the body and an expression of personal style and taste. In today's world, however, clothing can be much more than a fashion statement. It can provide protection and combat environmental problems that our planet faces.

- Sun-protective clothing is rated for its Ultraviolet Protection Factor (UPF)—the protection it offers against **UVA and UVB rays**. A fabric that is rated 50 allows only 1/50 of the sun's UV rays to penetrate it. The color, tightness of the weave, and weight of the fabric all affect its ability to block the sun's harmful rays. While some clothing does this naturally, like a heavy, dark-colored denim shirt, it isn't what you'd want to wear on a warm summer day. Clothing that is marketed as sun-protective is treated with chemical sunblock that absorbs UV rays. After many washings, it loses its effectiveness.

- Clothing that repels bugs is a recent trend for manufacturers of outdoor gear. Instead of slathering on smelly insect repellent, you can simply wear clothing that keeps the bugs away. Pyrethrin is a natural bug repellent found in certain species of chrysanthemum flowers. A **synthetic** form, called *permethrin*, is imbedded into a special fabric that is used for outdoor clothing. It is safe and odorless, but like sun-protective clothing, it is less effective after repeated washings.

- Most people don't consider clothing as being harmful to the environment. However, many synthetic fabrics, like polyester, are made from petroleum. There is a limited supply of petroleum, which is a fossil fuel, and drilling for it and processing it require energy. Even producing clothes from natural materials, like cotton, can have a negative impact. Twenty-five percent of pesticides used in the United States are applied to cotton fields to keep them free of insects and weeds.

New options in clothing are becoming available, and studies are underway to create even more choices. For example, **polymers** can be made from corn sugars and then woven into thread to create fabric. Clothing can be made of recycled materials, like soda bottles or the waste from cotton mills. Some companies offer clothing made from bamboo pulp, because unlike cotton, bamboo doesn't need a lot of pesticides to grow.

While we can't predict all the changes to come in clothing, one thing is for certain— the world of fashion won't ever be the same.

Write **true** or **false** next to each statement below.

1. _____ No clothing is sun-protective unless it contains a chemical sunblock.

2. _____ Both insect repellent clothing and sun-protective clothing are effective for only a limited number of washings.

3. _____ The most environmentally-responsible clothing is made of pure cotton.

4. _____ Clothing that is hydrophobic absorbs water.

5. _____ Nylon is an example of a synthetic material, while silk has a natural source.

Write your answers on the lines below.

6. Explain what role fossil fuels play in the creation of some fabrics.

_____

7. What effect do cotton crops have on the environment?

_____

_____

8. Why is bamboo potentially a good alternative to cotton?

_____

9. If you were asked to use science to create a new type of clothing, what would you make and why?

_____

_____

10. What benefits are there to making clothing out of recycled materials?

_____

_____

11. What purpose does each layer of extreme-weather clothing serve?

_____

_____

Creating a Healthier World

eradication: elimination

developing countries: countries that have a high level of poverty and low standard of living

immunizing: injecting with a vaccine in order to create immunity to an illness

"Our greatest concern must always rest with disadvantaged and vulnerable groups. These groups are often hidden, live in remote rural areas or shantytowns and have little political voice." —Dr. Margaret Chan, Director-General of WHO

In 2002 and 2003, an epidemic of a contagious respiratory disease called *SARS* infected more than 8,000 people and caused over 700 deaths. The outbreak originated in China, but the Chinese government did not inform WHO about it for several months— one reason why the disease spread to other countries. Once WHO became aware of the situation, they were able to set up procedures for dealing with patients, and implemented screenings at airports and quarantines to prevent further transmission.

Why is it necessary to have a global health agency?

The World Health Organization, known as WHO, is an agency of the United Nations. It began operating in 1948, three years after the formation of the UN. It has 193 member states and is headquartered in Geneva, Switzerland. Though the organization has many goals, its primary mission is to improve the health of people worldwide.

One of WHO's greatest accomplishments is the **eradication** of the smallpox virus. Smallpox is a highly contagious disease that is often fatal. Scientists believe that it first entered the human population more than 10,000 years ago when people began living in larger communities with the birth of agriculture. Because it is so easy to transmit, outbreaks of smallpox throughout history have wiped out large percentages of populations. This was particularly the case when Europeans arrived in the New World. After an aggressive vaccination campaign—with a focus on **developing countries**— WHO was able to declare that smallpox was eradicated in 1979. It was the first disease to be eliminated through human effort.

In addition to continuing efforts at **immunizing** people around the world, especially children, WHO's aim is to improve conditions that affect health— including sanitation, housing, nutrition, and working conditions. Poverty contributes to poor health, and poor health, in turn, prevents people from being able to pull themselves out of poverty. By working to make sure that people aren't denied access to health care or treatments because of their circumstances, WHO intends to break the cycle.

When AIDS was first identified in the early 1980s, WHO funded research to determine what caused the disease and how it was transmitted. Their research and search for a cure continues as they work to slow its spread. A great deal of incorrect information about its causes and how it is transmitted exist around the world. As a result, efforts by WHO and other organizations have focused on education, prevention, and counseling.

While rates have declined in some areas, they are still rising in others. About two-thirds of the people who currently have HIV (the virus that causes AIDS) live in sub-Saharan Africa. Combined with extreme poverty and the other health issues that exist there, the area is one of the neediest in the world. For these reasons, Dr. Margaret Chan, WHO's Director-General, has made the health of women and Africans a measure of the organization's success.

Circle the letter of the best answer to the question below.

1. Which of the following statements about WHO is not true?

   a. Vaccination of children around the world is one of WHO's priorities.

   b. WHO is an international organization, with representatives from nearly 200 nations.

   c. It is WHO's mission to help those who cannot help themselves.

   d. Because of WHO's vaccination campaign, SARS is no longer a threat.

Write your answers on the lines below.

2. How do you think that human beings' use of agriculture affected the spread of diseases?

   _____

3. What are two reasons why the eradication of smallpox was such a significant event?

   _____

   _____

4. If the primary goal of WHO is to improve health, why is the organization concerned with issues like housing, sanitation, and working conditions?

   _____

   _____

5. Why do you think it is important to have an international agency that deals with global health?

   _____

   _____

6. Why would the health of women and Africans be a measure or an indicator of the success of WHO?

   _____

   _____

7. Why is education an important part of WHO's mission? Be specific.

   _____

   _____

The Orbiting Junkyard

velocities: rates and directions of movement

deployment: the act of positioning something so that it is ready to be used

tethered: attached by a rope or cable

In 2007, astronaut Clay Anderson was assigned to take out the trash from the International Space Station. In a carefully planned maneuver, he was held away from the space station by a robotic arm, and then he pitched the junk at a precise angle that carried it away from the craft and toward the atmosphere. NASA is tracking this garbage and expects it to burn up sometime in 2008.

A wrench, a glove, cameras, and even a toothbrush are among the objects astronauts have lost during space walks.

In January 2007, a single explosion during the testing of a satellite created 1,900 pieces of space junk large enough to be tracked by radar.

What is space junk, and where does it come from?

Just as it does on Earth, human activity in space generates waste. Orbital debris, or "space junk," comes from many sources. Satellites are often abandoned once they're no longer useful. Spacecraft separations release nuts, bolts, and other parts into orbit, and astronauts lose tools that are awkward to hold with their bulky gloves. The majority of the junk, however, has been generated by more than 200 explosions that have occurred in space, usually as a result of testing new rockets or other spacecraft.

About 200 new pieces of space junk are added each year. This debris is not just slowly drifting through space. Space junk zips along at **velocities** ranging from a few hundred miles an hour up to 21,000 miles per hour. At those speeds, even small flecks of paint have been known to damage space shuttle windshields. In fact, more than 80 space shuttle windows have been replaced due to impacts with debris.

A lot of space junk eventually succumbs to Earth's gravitational pull and reenters the atmosphere. Like small meteorites, this debris usually burns up, but sometimes fragments survive. They often land in water, but large objects have also come close to hitting residential areas on land.

The U.S. Space Command tracks space junk by radar in order to avoid collisions with spacecraft. Even so, the equipment can only detect pieces larger than baseballs up to 600 miles high, and larger than volleyballs beyond that. In order to ensure the International Space Station has a clear path, NASA is investigating the use of high-powered lasers that could gently nudge pieces toward the atmosphere. Simply blasting the debris isn't an option because it would result in smaller particles that couldn't be tracked.

The best way to minimize the threat of space junk is not to create it. For example, **deployment** procedures can be used that don't require the ejection of objects, and tools can be **tethered** so that they don't drift away. A satellite can be designed to have a decaying orbit that slowly brings it into the atmosphere where it will burn up when it's no longer needed.

In recent years, an increasing number of satellites have been put into orbit as part of global communication systems. These satellites are vulnerable to impacts with pre-existing space junk, and any collision just creates more debris. The threat to astronauts and spacecraft—and even to people on the ground—has become a problem that can't be ignored.

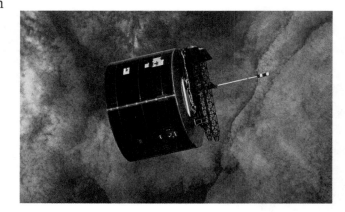

Circle the letter of the best answer to each question below.

1. NASA uses radar to track as much space junk as possible, but it's estimated that millions of pieces aren't being detected. Why?

   a. These pieces are too small.

   b. Junk that is made of metal reflects radio waves.

   c. NASA's radar covers only the area of space above North America.

   d. All of the above

2. Which of the following statements is true?

   a. All space debris completely disintegrates when it enters Earth's atmosphere.

   b. NASA is trying to use lasers to nudge debris out into open space.

   c. Space debris as small as a fleck of paint can be dangerous.

   d. Most space debris is created by astronauts who drop tools, bolts, or other objects.

Write your answers on the lines below.

3. Why does space junk eventually reenter Earth's atmosphere?

   _____

4. What causes debris to burn up when it enters Earth's atmosphere?

   _____

5. Why doesn't NASA just blow up old satellites or other space debris?

   _____

6. Why have more satellites been launched in recent years than in the past?

   _____

What's Next?

Skylab and Mir were two space stations that orbited Earth prior to the ISS. Skylab was launched by the United States and was in space from 1973 to 1979. The Russian space station Mir orbited from 1986 to 2001. At the conclusion of both missions, the stations were directed back into Earth's atmosphere, but neither one burned up completely. Do some research to determine where the pieces landed. Did they do any damage?

Ridding the World of Pests

beneficial: useful or helpful

biological amplification: the increase in concentrations of chemicals in organisms at higher levels of a food chain

organic: grown or raised without the use of pesticides, growth hormones, or antibiotics

Farmers, scientists, and consumers are becoming more aware of the hazards of pesticide use, and many are searching for alternative solutions. As a result, Integrated Pest Management (IPM) is becoming more and more widely used in the U.S. In this system, a variety of methods are used to control pests, including chemical, biological (such as the introduction of an insect's natural predators), and physical (such as removing weeds by hand). Controls made from more natural sources are also used. Pest populations are monitored carefully before pesticides are applied to determine whether they're necessary. When chemicals are used, an effort is made to choose ones that pose the least risk.

What are the pros and cons of using pesticides on farms?

Every year, the use of pesticides in U.S. agriculture prevents the loss of about nine billion dollars. Pesticides are chemicals used to control pests that have the potential to harm crops. The most common types are herbicides (to combat weeds), insecticides (to combat bugs), and fungicides (to combat fungus). Even with the use of a variety of control methods, about one-third of crops are still destroyed by pests.

Farmers, both the owners of small, family farms and the companies that own huge "agri-businesses," are hurt financially by the losses. Consumers are also affected when there is a shortage. Availability of certain items may decrease, and prices are certain to rise. Some people are able to pay the increased prices or have the luxury of choosing other foods. For many, however, food shortages can have serious consequences. Pesticides are an effective method of controlling the pests that damage crops.

Unfortunately, there is a high price to pay for the use of these chemicals. Pesticides are poison, and their effects aren't limited to the weeds and insects they target. One side effect is that **beneficial** populations can also be killed. For example, pesticides that target mosquitoes can also harm other "good" insects that feed on mosquitoes.

In addition, pesticides become a part of the groundwater when residues wash into the soil after it rains. Eventually, they end up polluting all our waterways. Not only can they harm the inhabitants of these waterways, but the effects can also become magnified higher up in the food chain—a concept known as **biological amplification**. The chemicals can affect overall health, as well as the reproduction of the affected animals.

It's probably no surprise, then, that pesticides are harmful to human beings, too. The people who have the greatest exposure—farmers and farm workers who harvest crops—are at the highest risk. They may experience a variety of health problems, including dizziness, vomiting, and respiratory difficulties. Even consumers can be at risk, which is one reason why it's so important to wash produce before you eat it. Most produce, as well as many other foods that use items like corn and soy, contain small amounts of pesticides. Organizations like the Environmental Protection Agency have determined that there is little health risk in consuming such small quantities of the chemicals. There are no guarantees, however, so some people choose to buy **organic** produce, which is grown naturally and pesticide free.

Write your answers on the lines below.

1. Why is the use of pesticides a complex issue?

    _____

    _____

2. Who is at the highest risk for exposure to pesticides?

    _____

3. What can you do to minimize the amount of pesticides you consume?

    _____

4. Give three examples of ways in which the use of pesticides harms the environment.

    _____

    _____

5. Explain what Integrated Pest Management is and why it's a step in the right direction as far as pesticide use is concerned.

    _____

    _____

Unifying Concepts and Processes

One problem with the use of pesticides is that over time they can stop being effective in killing insects or weeds. Explain what role natural selection plays in the development of immunity to certain chemicals.

_____

_____

_____

What's Next?

- Do some research to learn about writer/environmentalist Rachel Carson and her book *Silent Spring*. What effect did the book's publication have on the use of a pesticide called DDT?
- The use of pesticides can harm pollinators, like bees and butterflies. What effect does this have on the food supply? Go online or visit a library and learn what role pollinators play in producing the foods you eat every day.

Disaster on the Water

crude oil: oil before it is refined into gasoline and other petroleum products

hydrocarbons: chemical compounds made of only hydrogen and carbon; they form the backbone of crude oil

Human hair naturally absorbs oils. Using scrap hair from beauty salons is a cost-effective way to clean up oil after a spill.

On March 24, 1989, the *Exxon Valdez*, a supertanker carrying 42 million gallons of crude oil, ran into a reef off Alaska's southern coast. The resulting spill of more than 11 million gallons was one of the largest oil spills in U.S. history. About 250,000 marine birds were killed and 151 adult eagles were found dead. If the *Valdez* had a double hull, the spill would have been reduced by 60%. The cleanup cost was $2.1 billion and lasted four summers.

Cleanup crews save animals by using old-fashioned elbow grease. They wash the oil from the animals' eyes and clean their fur or feathers to break down the oil. Once clean, the animals are returned to their environments.

What happens after an oil spill?

After an oil spill, cleanup must begin quickly. Because oil and water don't mix, spilled **crude oil** floats on top of the water, creating an oil slick. As tides come in, the oil spreads over a larger area of water and is carried to land where it clings to the shore. This makes cleanup difficult.

There are several methods of cleaning spilled oil. Over time, it naturally biodegrades, but this is an impractical solution for large spills. Booms, which are like large rubber innertubes, contain the spill area and vacuum the oil. Sorbents—which are made of bales of straw, sawdust, minerals, or synthetic chemicals—act like giant sponges and are used to prevent oil from reaching the shoreline. Small boats called *skimmers* remove oil from the surface of the water, much like a vacuum.

Instead of removing the oil, dispersants chemically break it down into small droplets. They are often used on major oil spills when the oil is too thin to be absorbed or vacuumed. Dispersants, however, create additional problems because they can harm both animal and plant life.

Spilled oil can be burned off, but this causes air pollution. Burning spilled oil can also occur only when the water is calm because high winds may incite the fire.

On the beaches, workers use high-pressure hoses to wash the oil back into the water so that they can absorb or collect it there. Vacuum trucks drive along the beaches to vacuum the oil from the sand.

Hydrocarbons are a risk to marine plants and animals following an oil spill. Birds can be smothered or drowned by the oil. It also causes their feathers to stick together, which makes them unable to fly. Mammals with fur, like sea otters, die from ingesting oil during grooming. It also prevents them from maintaining a sufficient body temperature, which means they can freeze to death. Animals that aren't immediate victims of oil spills are still at risk for developing related problems. Even low doses of hydrocarbons can harm vision, smell, growth, reproduction, and the ability to hunt.

There are many efficient and effective methods for humans to clean up oil spills, but oil-related damage still occurs every year. The best way to decrease the effects of oil spills is to prevent them.

Circle the letter of the best answer to each question below.

1. Which of the following is not a method of cleaning up after an oil spill?

   a. booms

   b. hulls

   c. skimmers

   d. dispersants

2. Which of the following statements is true?

   a. Although cleanup is expensive and time consuming, there are no real long-term effects of an oil spill.

   b. Once animals have contact with large quantities of oil, they cannot be saved.

   c. Oil tankers that have double hulls are likely to spill less oil in an accident.

   d. Burning spilled oil is a safe option only on windy days.

Write your answers on the lines below.

3. What kind of long-term problems can hydrocarbons cause for animals?

   _____

4. The *Exxon Valdez* oil spill had an enormous impact on local birds. How might the changes in bird populations have affected other animals in the ecosystem?

   _____

   _____

5. If crude oil will eventually biodegrade, why are immediate cleanup efforts necessary after a major spill?

   _____

   _____

Unifying Concepts and Processes

Review Lesson 5.2. Then, explain how biotechnology could be used in the cleanup effort after an oil spoil.

_____

_____

exclusion zone: the 30-kilometer area surrounding the Chernobyl disaster site; people were originally banned from it, but today, some have returned there to live at their own risk

sarcophagus: the concrete container that prevents radiation leaks from the damaged Chernobyl reactor

More than 100 radioactive elements were released when the reactor exploded. Most had short half-lives and decayed quickly. However, isotopes of strontium-90 and caesium-137 are still found in the area because they have half-lives of 29 and 30 years.

It's difficult to estimate how many people died as a result of the accident because it's hard to know which cases of cancer were caused by the radiation. The best estimates today state that in addition to the 56 people who died immediately following the accident, another 9,000 of the 6.5 million exposed have died or will die as a result of the radiation.

How did the nuclear disaster at Chernobyl happen?

In early morning on April 26, 1986, a test was run on Reactor 4 at the nuclear power plant in Chernobyl, Ukraine—a part of the former USSR. The reactor was running at low power, which made it unstable. Safety precautions that should have been followed by the operators were ignored. As a result, a massive steam explosion took place. It led to a fire in the reactor, causing radiation to be released into the air. The reactor should have been housed in a concrete and steel structure, but it wasn't. Instead, Chernobyl became the worst nuclear power disaster in history.

No one seemed to know immediately how extensive the damage was or how dangerous the conditions were. Firefighters weren't alerted to the danger and didn't wear protective gear. Many of the firefighters and cleanup workers died from exposure to radiation.

In total, about 200,000 nearby residents were evacuated in the weeks after the accident. Radioactive particles were carried on wind currents and traveled across Scandinavia, Europe, and the United Kingdom. The level of radiation in many countries was briefly above normal, but the effects weren't long lasting and no health issues have been tied to it. The Ukraine, Belarus, and Russia were the hardest hit. In particular, the 30-kilometer (18-mile) area that surrounded the nuclear plant became known as the **exclusion zone** and still remains mostly uninhabited today.

Following the accident, something had to be done to quickly stop the additional spreading of radiation. A **sarcophagus** was quickly constructed of concrete to encase the entire reactor. Some of the construction was even done with industrial robots to reduce the amount of human contact. Because it was built so quickly, though, it hasn't held up very well during the last 20 years. It's badly in need of repairs or replacement. Collapse would mean that the remaining radioactive material in the reactor could escape.

It can be hard to see any positive outcomes from such a large-scale tragedy, but there are some. Although some mutations were seen in local animals after the accident, in recent years, animals like moose, wolves, and beavers are returning to the region. The near absence of human beings in the area is creating a sort of unexpected nature preserve.

Write **true** or **false** next to each statement below.

1. _____ Within three months of the accident, most residents returned to their homes in the exclusion zone.

2. _____ The effects of the accident were felt around Europe and Scandinavia.

3. _____ Design and operation problems were the cause of the explosion.

Write your answers on the lines below.

4. What was the purpose of constructing the sarcophagus?

_____

5. What problems exist with the sarcophagus today?

_____

6. Why isn't there a good way to determine how many deaths were caused by the accident?

_____

_____

7. Explain what effect the accident has had on the local animal populations. If more humans return to the area one day, do you predict there will be more changes for local wildlife?

_____

_____

Unifying Concepts and Processes

Review the portion of Lesson 1.4 that deals with radiometric dating and half-lives. If caesium-137 has a

half-life of 30 years, how long will it take for three-quarters of it to decay? _____

What's Next?

Although there are obviously some serious risks to using nuclear power, there are also many benefits. Do some research online or at the library to find out why nuclear power is often a smart energy choice. Then, form your own opinion—are the benefits worth the risks?

Review

Circle the letter of the best answer to each question below.

1. How much water do you need when you're exercising?

   a. about 32 ounces before and after you exercise

   b. about 8 ounces every 20 minutes

   c. about 8 ounces every hour

   d. about 24 ounces every half hour

2. Which of the following is the FDA not responsible for?

   a. household cleansers

   b. cosmetics

   c. products that emit radiation

   d. pharmaceutical drugs

3. What usually happens to space junk that reenters Earth's atmosphere?

   a. It explodes, breaking into pieces that are too tiny to be problematic.

   b. No one knows for sure.

   c. It is detected by NASA's radar and recaptured.

   d. It burns up.

Write your answers on the lines below.

4. What are two effective ways of dealing with stress?

   _____

5. Give three examples of symptoms that may be stress related.

   _____

6. Are supplements a good source of nutrition for athletes? Explain.

   _____

7. What is the purpose of the FDA?

   _____

8. Why is poverty such a concern for WHO?

   _____

9. How can the material of the clothing you choose to wear affect the environment?

_____

_____

10. Why is space junk a problem?

_____

11. Explain one pro and one con for the use of pesticides in farming.

_____

_____

12. Why do you think Integrated Pest Management is becoming more widely used?

_____

_____

13. How do oil spills affect animals?

_____

_____

Write **true** or **false** next to each statement below.

14. _____ Stress can have both positive and negative effects on your life.

15. _____ Athletes need more protein in their diets than non-athletes do.

16. _____ Eating lots of meats and fatty foods before an athletic event is called *carbo-loading*.

17. _____ Clothing for extremely cold conditions includes layers that have different functions.

18. _____ Tuberculosis was the first disease to be eradicated by WHO.

19. _____ Explosions in space are the greatest source of space junk.

Lesson 7.1   Exploring the Silent World

SCUBA: an acronym for *self-contained underwater breathing apparatus*

documentary: a nonfiction film that presents footage of actual people, places, or events

submersible: an undersea vehicle that is used for exploring the ocean or performing specific tasks

"From birth, man carries the weight of gravity on his shoulders. He is bolted to the earth. But man has only to sink beneath the surface and he is free. Buoyed by water, he can fly in any direction—up, down, sideways—by merely flipping his hand."
—Jacques Yves Cousteau

Among its many unique features, *Calypso* had an observation chamber with eight portholes that allowed the crew to observe the goings-on underwater. In 1996, *Calypso* was damaged by a barge in Singapore and sank. Although Cousteau died in 1997, expeditions continue today in *Alcyone*, meaning "daughter of the wind."

Cousteau made more than 100 films and authored 50 books.

What contributions did Jacques Cousteau make to the study of the world's oceans?

The oceans have always been a source of mystery for human beings. Though there is still a lot to learn, much of what we know today can be traced to history's most renowned ocean explorer—Jacques Cousteau.

Even the best early diving equipment didn't allow much freedom because it kept the diver anchored to the surface via an air tube. In 1943, Cousteau solved the problem by inventing the Aqua-Lung, an early form of **SCUBA**, with an engineer named Emil Gagnan. Using the Aqua-Lung, a diver could breathe compressed air from a cylinder and remain underwater longer.

In 1950, Cousteau purchased a former World War II minesweeper and had it customized. For the next 40 years, *Calypso* took Cousteau on expeditions to nearly every major body of water. The crew's motto was always "We must go see for ourselves."

In doing so, Cousteau and his crew photographed and gathered samples of plant and animal life that had never before been seen. Cousteau's greatest contribution, however, was bringing appreciation of the oceans to the public. In 1955, his award-winning **documentary** *The Silent World*, was released and people became fascinated by an inside-look deep underwater. By showing the world the beauty and diversity of ocean life, he gave people a reason to find it worth preserving.

The invention of the Aqua-Lung wasn't Cousteau's only contribution to ocean exploration equipment. He also helped invent a diving saucer—a small **submersible** that could carry two passengers to depths of about 1,150 feet. It had movable lights to illuminate the deep-sea darkness, as well as a robotic arm used for gathering samples. Two smaller versions of the diving saucer, nicknamed "sea fleas," were launched in 1967. The single passenger vehicles were easier to maneuver and could dive about 1,640 feet.

Perhaps the most interesting of Cousteau's endeavors were the three Conshelf experiments. These underwater structures allowed "oceanauts" to live underwater. The living quarters were equipped with TVs, radios, and beds. The oceanauts lived, exercised, and worked underwater. The effects on their health were studied, much the way today's astronauts are studied. The experiments showed that people could live underwater, but it was concluded that human beings aren't meant to live without sun.

Circle the letter of the best answer to the question below.

1. How was the Aqua-Lung different from early diving apparatus?

   a. It was heavier and bulkier but less expensive.

   b. It allowed the diver more freedom.

   c. It allowed the diver to breath without being connected to air tubes at the surface.

   d. Both b and c

Write your answers on the lines below.

2. What role do you think Cousteau's experiences as an oceanographer played in his inventions?

   _____

   _____

3. Explain the importance of Cousteau's films.

   _____

   _____

4. How is deep sea exploration similar to space exploration?

   _____

   _____

5. If more underwater communities like Conshelf had been built, what do you think the effects on the ocean might have been? Do you think that this would have contributed to efforts aimed at ocean preservation, or would the results have been the opposite? Explain.

   _____

   _____

   _____

What's Next?

Today, the Cousteau Society carries on the work of Jacques Cousteau. Do some research to learn more about the society and their goals and expeditions.

Bering land bridge: a land bridge approximately 1,000 miles long that joined Siberia and Alaska during the ice ages of the Pleistocene

Radiocarbon dating had originally been done on many of the Clovis artifacts in the 1960s and 70s. Methods and technology have improved quite a bit since then. During the current series of dating, Waters obtained samples of bones from many Clovis sites. He and his partner, Thomas Stafford, used collagen they extracted from the bones. By putting this through a molecular sieve, they were able to test and date pure amino acids (the building blocks of protein) from the bones.

Who were the first people to arrive and settle in the Americas?

For about half a century, it was believed that the Clovis were the first group of people to inhabit the Americas. They were named after Clovis, New Mexico—the area where the artifacts attributed to them were found in 1933. The first spearhead was quite a discovery because it indicated that its creators could make and use weapons. It was found near the skeleton of a mammoth, and later spearheads were found mixed in with mammoth remains—leading scientists to the conclusion that these ancient people had hunted some very large game.

After the initial discovery of the Clovis artifacts in New Mexico, hundreds of other Clovis spearheads were found scattered all across the United States and down into Central and South America. The artifacts were dated at about 11,500 years old. No older traces of human existence had been found in these areas, so archaeologists concluded that the Clovis were the first Americans.

It is accepted in the scientific community that the earliest human ancestors originated in Africa. Over tens of thousands of years, they spread out over Europe, Asia, and Australia. Scientists believed that the Clovis journeyed over the **Bering land bridge**, and then spread throughout the Americas, eventually reaching the southern tip of South America about 1,000 years after their arrival.

Over the years, parts of the "Clovis First" theory began to crumble. For example, in several places, human artifacts had been found that appeared to be older than those made by the Clovis. As a result, a study was done to examine the Clovis artifacts again and to date them using newer, more accurate methods. After dating artifacts from more than 25 North American sites, the researchers were surprised to learn that the Clovis had arrived about 400 years later than originally believed. In addition, the Clovis appeared to have existed for only about 200 years. This makes it unlikely that they would have been able to spread so far in such a short period of time.

Currently, Michael Waters (the lead scientist on the project) believes that America became populated by several different groups of people. They probably arrived at different times and by different means—even including boats. This idea would replace the theory that the first Americans arrived in a single event. Now, the search begins to find out who the first Americans were, when they arrived, and how they got here.

Circle the letter of the best answer to each question below.

1. The earliest ancestors of modern human beings lived in

   a. Australia.

   b. Europe.

   c. Africa.

   d. the Americas.

2. The Clovis were believed to be the first Americans because

   a. materials at their sites were dated at more than 40,000 years old.

   b. evidence of older American cultures hadn't yet been found.

   c. no evidence of interaction with other groups of people had been found.

   d. Both a and b

Write your answers on the lines below.

3. What is the current theory about the arrival of the first Americans?

   _____

   _____

4. How did archaeologists determine the use of Clovis spearheads?

   _____

5. The "Clovis First" theory was accepted as true for many years. Why was it necessary to start investigating the first Americans again?

   _____

6. The next step in solving the mystery will be for archaeologists to re-date the artifacts that they believe are older than the Clovis ones. Why is this important?

   _____

   _____

Unifying Concepts and Processes

Give one example from this selection of deductive or inductive reasoning.

   _____

solstice: either of the two times each year when the sun is farthest from the equator; the summer solstice is the day with the longest period of sunlight, and the winter solstice is the shortest

equinox: either of the two times each year when the sun is closest to the equator, and day and night are of equal length

archeoastronomers: archeologists who study the astronomical knowledge of ancient cultures and the sites they built

Anasazi: an ancient Native American culture located in the Southwest; also known as the *Ancient Pueblo People*

cairn: a mound of stones used as a marker

Maya: a powerful, highly-developed civilization in Central America that reached its peak about 1,500 years ago

solar year: the time it takes Earth to complete one orbit of the sun

synchronized: work in unison; occur at the same rate

What did the original inhabitants of the Americas know about astronomy?

Deep in the Utah desert, an ancient brick structure sits quietly in the sun. Although some sections of wall have crumbled into piles of stone, much of it still stands tall. Named *Hovenweep Castle* for its resemblance to a medieval fortress, this prehistoric building encloses a special space. Holes were placed in the exterior walls so that at sunset on a **solstice** or **equinox**, sunlight streams into the room and falls onto doorways within the structure. **Archeoastronomers** assume that the **Anasazi** constructed these "sun rooms" to mark the longest and shortest days of the year.

Like many other ancient peoples, the earliest Americans made careful observation of celestial objects an important part of their culture. Understanding when and where the sun, moon, stars, and planets appeared during the year helped them track time.

It's difficult to date stone structures precisely, but the Anasazi culture is known to have peaked about 1,000 years ago, so the sun rooms were most likely built then as well. Some of the oldest monuments in the Americas, however, would certainly have to be medicine wheels. Some of these circular stone structures are 4,000 or more years old. The Bighorn Medicine Wheel in Wyoming, with a diameter of nearly 80 feet, is one of the largest examples.

A large pile of stones, called a **cairn**, sits at the center of the Bighorn Wheel, while 28 lines of rocks resembling spokes stretch to the wheel's outer rim. Just beyond the rim are six smaller piles of stones. During the summer solstice, the sun rises directly over the central cairn if you're standing on a particular pile. Some of the rock lines point directly at spots on the horizon where bright stars, such as Sirius and Rigel, rise at certain times of the year.

The most precise timekeepers of ancient America were probably the **Maya**. They combined an advanced mathematical system with their detailed knowledge of astronomy to create one of history's most accurate calendars.

The Maya calendar actually consists of two calendars used in combination. One is based on a **solar year**—it has 365 days. The other has only 260 days per year. Because the two calendars use years of different lengths, they aren't **synchronized**. It takes a cycle 52 solar years before Day 1 of one calendar matches up again with Day 1 in the other calendar. In other words, for 52 years, every single day has a unique name!

Write your answers on the lines below.

1. Explain the difference between a solstice and an equinox.

_____

_____

2. How did the Anasazi sun room function?

_____

_____

3. Why would tracking time be such an important part of ancient life? Give specific examples.

_____

_____

4. The Maya didn't understand that Earth traveled through space and circled the sun once every 365 days. However, they were still able to determine that this was the length of a solar year. Explain in as much detail as possible how you think they were able to do it.

_____

_____

_____

Unifying Concepts and Processes

According to the selection, were relative or absolute dating methods used to determine the age of the Anasazi sun room?

_____

What's Next?

There are ancient observatories and astronomical sites located all over the world. Do some research to learn more about Hovenweep, medicine wheels, Stonehenge, and other sites.

genome: the complete genetic information contained in chromosomes, including genes and DNA sequences

geneticists: biologists who specialize in the study of genes

DNA sequencers: instruments that use lasers and fluorescent dyes to determine the chemical sequences in DNA fragments

base pairs: the pairs of chemicals that connect the two halves of a molecule of DNA

algorithms: series of clear instructions performed in specific sequences in order to reach conclusions that are usually mathematical

Everyone, except identical twins, has a unique genetic sequence. The Human Genome Project focused on the DNA from just four individuals. The next step is to compare genomes from different people and discover which parts of the sequence correspond to specific genetic information.

In 1980, Frederick Sanger and Walter Gilbert were awarded the Nobel Prize in chemistry for their work in DNA sequencing.

How did scientists break the chemical code in our DNA?

The Human **Genome** Project is as one of the greatest scientific achievements in history. An international team of **geneticists**, mathematicians, computer specialists, and other scientists worked together to crack the code buried within our DNA. Thanks to specially-designed **DNA sequencers**, and supercomputers that could analyze the data, the human genome was mapped much more quickly than anyone ever imagined.

After James Watson and Francis Crick discovered the structure of DNA molecules, scientists began analyzing the sequence of chemical bonds that form them. A DNA molecule consists of just four chemicals that pair up in specific combinations. These pairs join together into long DNA chains, and the order in which they combine forms genes—the coded instructions for each cell in every living organism. Genetic information is stored and processed in a way similar to a computer's binary number system, using a system of **base pairs** formed from just four chemicals.

The first complete genome was mapped in the early 1970s. It was the relatively simple genetic sequence of a virus—about 5,000 chemical units in length. A couple of years later, English biochemist Frederick Sanger developed a technique to determine the sequence of another virus.

Sanger's "Shotgun Sequencing" technique breaks two identical DNA strands into millions of random pieces. The individual fragments of each strand are analyzed to determine the base pair sequences they contain, and then the data is fed into a computer. The computer uses complex **algorithms** to compare the pieces from each strand, and then reassembles the information to show the chemical sequence of the entire strand.

This technique worked for bacteria and other simple organisms, but could it work for the human genome? The human genome contains a DNA sequence three billion base pairs long. When it was announced in the early 1990s that a serious attempt would be made to map this sequence, many scientists thought the task would be impossible. Its success relied heavily on how quickly the project's computers could process information.

Throughout the 1990s, computer technology improved dramatically, and a fierce competition began between two groups of scientists trying to map the human genome first. In early 2000, the leaders of the two projects announced to the public that they had accomplished this amazing goal.

Circle the letter of the best answer to the question below.

1. DNA base pairs are formed from

   a. just four different chemicals.

   b. billions of different chemicals.

   c. chromosomes.

   d. Both a and c

Write your answers on the lines below.

2. Why were computers such an important part of the Human Genome Project?

   _____

   _____

3. Briefly describe what a DNA sequencer does.

   _____

   _____

4. In 1990, a publicly-funded project was initiated to map the human genome. In 1998, one of its leading scientists left to lead a similar, competing project funded by a private company. Explain how competition between these two groups helped speed up the mapping process.

   _____

   _____

5. The private company that was racing to map the human genome wanted to place patents on many of the genes they discovered. A patent is a legal document that gives the owner exclusive rights to use an invention, a discovery, or an idea. In 2000, President Bill Clinton declared that the human genome sequence could not be patented. If only one company or individual was allowed to patent certain parts of the human genome, what effect do you think this would have had on science?

   _____

   _____

When Cotton Became King

bolls: cotton seedpods

cash crop: a crop grown for profit, not just for home use

In 1798, the U.S. government offered contracts to anyone who could make muskets for their upcoming war with the French. The manufacture of guns was a slow and tedious process because they were all made by hand. Although it was not an original idea, Eli Whitney implemented the use of interchangeable parts to mass-produce weapons. He made standardized parts and assembled them all at the end. This idea sped up the manufacturing process because it meant that one bolt was as good as the next. Factories quickly adopted Whitney's methods of production. Today, this can be seen in everything from the manufacturing of cars to microchips.

How did the cotton gin revolutionize agriculture?

In 1793, about 10,000 bales of cotton were harvested in the United States. Less than 70 years later, just prior to the Civil War, 5 million bales of cotton were harvested, and 75 percent of the world's cotton was produced in America. What increased cotton production so dramatically?

As a young man, Eli Whitney visited a friend's plantation in Georgia. The owners were having trouble cleaning cotton efficiently. The seeds of the green cotton plant were sticky and had to be removed from the **bolls** before the cotton could be used to make fabric. This was a time-consuming process, and a worker, usually a slave, could clean only about one pound per day.

Whitney quickly realized that a machine could accelerate the process. After only a few short days, he built a cotton gin. It was a simple device in which a wire screen held the cotton while a drum with hooks turned. The cotton was fed past the hooks, which picked the seeds out. The cotton passed through, but the seeds were stopped. The cotton gin made it possible to clean 50 pounds of cotton per day. Whitney's amazing invention helped to begin the American Industrial Revolution.

With the cleaning time shortened, cotton became the **cash crop** of the Southern United States, and it revived the economy of the region. With the abundance of cotton, other machines were invented to use the increased yield of the crop. Francis C. Lowell combined the process of spinning and weaving cotton into one factory, which quickly milled bolts of fabric. Elias Howe perfected a sewing machine that mimicked his wife's hand sewing. Suddenly, with the cotton gin and the sewing machine, clothing could be produced efficiently in factories rather than at home.

Whitney's invention led to the growth of the agriculture-based economy of the South. In the years after the invention of the cotton gin, other inventors followed Whitney's lead in developing equipment to mechanize farming. For example, in 1831, Cyrus McCormick developed the mechanical reaper to harvest grain. The combined harvester and thresher, or combine, was introduced in 1836 to cut grain and thresh it from the straw. John Deere invented the steel plow in 1837.

Eli Whitney showed that the power of an inventive mind and the desire to solve a problem could change the face of American agriculture—and ultimately, American history.

Use the words in the box to complete the sentences below.

mechanized	manufacturing	combine	efficiently	interchangeable

1. The invention of the _____ allowed farmers to use a single machine to cut grain and thresh it from the straw.

2. The use of _____ parts allows products to be mass-produced.

3. The invention of the cotton gin, the steel plow, and the combine are all example of ways in which

   farming became _____.

4. Whitney seemed to have an innate ability to find ways in which work could be done

   more _____.

5. Whitney's ideas and inventions changed both American agriculture and _____.

Write your answers on the lines below.

6. What problem did the invention of Whitney's cotton gin solve?

   _____

7. The invention of the cotton gin increased the amount of cotton that could be cleaned each day by

   _____ times.

8. How does a cotton gin work?

   _____

   _____

9. What effect did the sudden increase in the supply of cotton have on technology of the time?

   _____

   _____

What's Next?

Slavery, the cotton industry, and the South will be forever intertwined in American history. Find out what effect the invention of the cotton gin had on slavery. Did it do the work of slaves, making them less necessary? Or did the larger crop sizes increase a plantation owner's need for slaves?

personal computers: small and relatively inexpensive computers used by individuals

abacus: a device with sliding beads or balls that is used to make calculations

punch cards: cards with holes in specific positions and patterns; the holes represent information that is used to control a machine

software: a set of instructions that control the operations of a computer

ENIAC: acronym for *electronic numeral integrator and computer*

integrated circuit: a device made up of electrical parts, such as transistors, that are etched or imprinted onto a tiny slice of semiconducting material, like silicon

microprocessor: a single integrated circuit that controls all of the information in a computer

Valley

Who was the first person to design a machine that could calculate numbers?

Computers are common sights today, but it was only about 30 years ago that the first **personal computers** hit the market. The history of computers stretches back much farther than that, though. This timeline highlights a few important historical moments in the development of computer technologies.

circa 3,000 B.C.—The **abacus** was developed in China.

1623—Wilhelm Schickard used timekeeping technology to create a "calculating clock." Instead of telling time, the gears and other moving parts were used to add and subtract numbers up to six digits long.

1670—Gottfried von Leibniz unveiled his more complex version of a mechanical calculator. It added and subtracted, but it also multiplied and divided. Leibniz was also the first to describe the binary number system.

1801—Joseph-Marie Jacquard designed a loom that used **punch cards**. Each card had a unique arrangement of holes and controlled which patterns the machine would weave. These cards are the first examples of **software**.

1833—Charles Babbage used Jacquard's punch card technology to design what many consider to be the first computer. Babbage's machine could perform complex mathematical calculations. It was also a printer and could create new punch cards. Although this machine was never actually built, Babbage is still known as the "father of computing."

1842—While translating a description of Babbage's machine into Italian, Ada Lovelace wrote a detailed description of how a specific series of punch cards could be used to reach a particular mathematical conclusion. Some historians consider her instructions to be the first computer program.

1939—Konrad Zuse created the Z3. It was the first electric, programmable computer that used a binary number system. The same year, John Atanasoff designed the first electronic computer that could process digital information.

1946—**ENIAC** was put to use by the Army. It was about 1,000 times faster than any other computer, and it could perform a variety of functions.

1947—The transistor was developed.

1951—UNIVAC 1 became the first computer sold to the public.

1959—The **integrated circuit**, or microchip, was invented.

1966—Hand-held calculators became possible because of microchips.

1968—The **microprocessor** was developed by Ted Hoff. Microprocessors and microchips shrunk computers down considerably, and the era of personal computers was born.

Circle the letter of the best answer to each question below.

1. What is an abacus?

   a. a device used to make mathematical calculations

   b. the first powerful computer used by the U.S. Army

   c. the first computer sold to the public

   d. a loom that is controlled by punch cards

2. Ada Lovelace

   a. created the first computer software.

   b. wrote the first computer program.

   c. developed punch cards for Babbage's computing machine.

   d. designed a printer to be used with Babbage's machine.

Write your answers on the lines below.

3. Why are punch cards considered a form of software?

   _____

   _____

   _____

4. Which two inventions allowed computers to become small enough to be practical for use by the public at large?

   _____   _____

Unifying Concepts and Processes

Calculators and computers both manipulate numbers, but computers are more versatile because they can be reprogrammed. Computers can manipulate just about any piece of information, but what has to happen to the information first?

   _____

   _____

Lise Meitner: Mother of the Atomic Age

radioactivity: the emission of particles of matter and energy from the nuclei of unstable isotopes

isotopes: the different atoms of an element that all have equal numbers of protons but different numbers of neutrons

Manhattan Project: a secret United States government program, begun in 1942, with the purpose of developing an atomic bomb

Although the Nobel Prize committee ignored her contributions, Meitner won plenty of other awards in her life, including the National Women's Press Club's Woman of the Year in 1946, the Max Planck Medal from the German Physics Society in 1949, and the U.S. Department of Energy's Enrico Fermi Award in 1966.

The element *Meitnerium*, created in 1982, was named in Meitner's honor.

Who was the woman Albert Einstein called the "German Marie Curie"?

Lise Meitner was one of the 20th century's greatest physicists. Born in Vienna, Austria, she earned her doctorate in physics in 1906. Meitner knew that in Vienna the only work available to a female scientist would be teaching. She was more interested in research, so she headed to Berlin, Germany. Soon, she met another great physicist, Otto Hahn, and the two began a 30-year collaboration studying **radioactivity** and **isotopes**.

When Meitner and Hahn started their research, neutrons hadn't yet been discovered. Around 1930, though, scientists saw that the heavy nuclei of isotopes were stuffed with these neutral particles. A competition among scientists began to see who could add even more neutrons to an isotope's nucleus first.

Meanwhile, many changes were occurring in Germany. In 1933, Adolph Hitler came to power. Jewish scientists were forced to resign their positions, and most left the country. Meitner was Jewish, but she was an Austrian citizen and was allowed to keep her job. She and Hahn continued their work, but when Austria was invaded and became part of Germany five years later, Meitner's citizenship no longer mattered. In 1938, she fled to Sweden.

Meitner and Hahn continued their research, meeting secretly in Denmark. Their work led them to a startling conclusion. Hahn wasn't convinced, but Meitner was sure that bombarding the uranium isotopes with neutrons caused the nuclei to break apart. In 1939, Meitner published a paper explaining how the uranium nucleus split and formed two lighter elements, releasing a large amount of energy. Meitner called the process *nuclear fission*.

Meitner went on to describe the tremendous explosive power that would result from a nuclear fission chain reaction—knowledge that she knew Hahn and other scientists in Nazi Germany had as well. Because of Meitner's paper, Albert Einstein wrote to President Roosevelt to warn him that this dangerous knowledge was in Nazi hands. The **Manhattan Project** was soon underway. It was assumed that Meitner would be one of the project's leaders, but she refused to have anything to do with the creation of a bomb.

After World War II ended, Meitner criticized Hahn and other German scientists who hadn't spoken out against the Nazis. In 1945, Hahn alone was awarded a Nobel Prize for his work with nuclear fission, but other prominent physicists of the time vigorously defended Meitner's contributions. Today, her place in scientific history is assured.

Circle the letter of the best answer to each question below.

1. Lisa Meitner helped discover

    a. isotopes.

    b. radioactivity.

    c. nuclear fission.

    d. All of the above

2. Why were Hahn and Meitner bombarding nuclei with neutrons in the first place?

    a. They wanted to see if protons in a nucleus would repel neutrons.

    b. They were trying to add more neutrons to an isotope's nucleus.

    c. They thought neutrons might slow down the rate of radioactive decay.

    d. They were looking for evidence of quarks.

Write your answers on the lines below.

3. What was the purpose of the Manhattan Project?

    _____

4. Why didn't Meitner remain in Vienna after she received her doctorate?

    _____

Unifying Concepts and Processes

Explain the role ethics played in Meitner's decision not to join the Manhattan Project.

_____

_____

What's Next?

Lise Meitner may have criticized Otto Hahn's actions during the war, but she never questioned his brilliance as a scientist, or the fact that he deserved the Nobel Prize in chemistry. Hahn spent the remainder of his life speaking out against the misuse of nuclear power, and it was repeatedly suggested that he be nominated for a Nobel Peace Prize.

Hurtling into Space

A space shuttle consists of the main spacecraft, called the *orbiter*, and its support systems—known together as a *Space Transportation System* (STS). For the shuttle to leave Earth's atmosphere, an enormous amount of thrust is necessary. Two rocket boosters give the shuttle this power for the first two minutes, taking it to an altitude of 28 miles at a speed of about 3,100 miles per hour. Then, the two boosters disattach from the STS and fall into the ocean. They are retrieved by a NASA team and prepared for use in future flights.

A shuttle's external fuel tank uses 500,000 gallons of fuel during its eight minutes of service at the beginning of a flight.

Why were the first space shuttles developed?

The earliest manned space vehicles were used for only a single mission. They cost millions of dollars to build but were essentially disposable. In the 1970s, NASA set to work designing and constructing the first space shuttle. Unlike its earlier relatives, it could be used for about 100 flights.

In January 1972, President Nixon gave the following statement: *"I have decided today that the United States should proceed at once with the development of an entirely new type of space transportation system. . . . It will revolutionize transportation into near space, by routinizing it. . . . In the scientific arena, the past decade of experience has taught us that spacecraft are an irreplaceable tool for learning about our near-Earth space environment, the Moon, and the planets, besides being an important aid to our studies of the Sun and stars. . . . This is why commitment to the Space Shuttle program is the right step for America to take."* Today, the shuttle remains the most technologically complex machine human beings have created.

A space shuttle is capable of transporting seven or eight crewmembers to and from orbit around Earth. It carries payload, or equipment, into space in a huge cargo bay. The payload might be a smaller spacecraft, materials for conducting experiments, satellites and their repair materials, or parts and supplies for the International Space Station. The cargo bay can also serve as a work area for the crew as they make repairs or conduct experiments.

Columbia, the first U.S. space shuttle, was ready for flight in 1981. It carried two crewmembers, and its first mission lasted only two days. *Columbia* completed 28 missions and spent 300 days in space.

In January of 2003, the shuttle took off with a crew of seven who planned to perform experiments in microgravity. During the launch, a piece of insulation foam hit the wing, creating a small hole. When the shuttle attempted reentry into Earth's atmosphere, hot gases entered the wing. The shuttle quickly burned up, killing the crew.

This disaster, as well as the loss of the shuttle *Challenger* and its crew in 1986, stunned the nation. People felt emotionally invested in the space program and the astronauts. The two tragic disasters are a reminder of the risks of space travel. After 135 flights, the Space Shuttle program was retired in 2011, with the launch of Atlantis.

Match each term in column 1 with its description in column 2. Write the letter of your answer on the line.

1. _____ rocket boosters   **a.** the part of the spacecraft that carries the crew

2. _____ external fuel tank   **b.** carries the payload

3. _____ payload   **c.** responsible for providing thrust at liftoff

4. _____ cargo bay   **d.** provides the material needed to produce the shuttle's power

5. _____ orbiter   **e.** equipment

Write your answers on the lines below.

6. Why did President Nixon encourage the development of NASA's space shuttle program? Be specific.

_____

_____

7. What was the main way in which space shuttles were different from the manned space vehicles that came before them?

_____

8. Give three examples of tasks that crewmembers might perform while on a mission.

_____

_____

9. Reread the last paragraph of the selection. Do you believe that human beings will continue to explore space despite the risks? If so, do you agree with the author's reasons why?

_____

_____

What's Next?

Do some research to find out what took the space shuttle's will take their place. What are the advantages to the replacement system? Is it safer? Less expensive? What happened to the retired shuttles?

An Introduction to Special Relativity

constant: a number that expresses a property or quantity that doesn't change

Here are some of the other important ideas contained in Einstein's Special Theory:

- Space and time aren't separate things. They are a single quantity called *space-time*. Time is the fourth dimension beyond height, width, and depth.

- Mass and energy are interchangeable. In other words, mass can be converted into energy, and energy can be converted into mass. The formula for this change is $E=MC^2$, or energy equals mass times the speed of light squared.

- Because the speed of light doesn't change, time and mass have to change if an object approaches the speed of light. To an observer, the object's mass will increase and time will slow down.

Why is the speed of light such an important part of physics?

Sir Isaac Newton published his laws of motion and gravity in 1687, and for 200 years, physicists used them to explain how matter moved through the universe. Newton's simple rules lay behind every physical action physicists observed, and many scientists thought there wasn't a lot left to explain about physics. Then, in 1887, a single experiment changed everything.

The discovery of electromagnetism had allowed scientists to see how light energy moves through space as waves. Physicists assumed that, like waves in water, electromagnetic waves moved through some kind of **medium** as well. In 1887, Albert Michelson and Edward Morley designed an experiment that would detect this invisible medium by comparing the speeds of two light beams moving in different directions. They spent lots of money and time developing increasingly precise equipment, but they couldn't detect a difference in speed between the two beams.

Many physicists assumed that the experiments still weren't precise enough or done carefully enough. Young Albert Einstein, however, decided that the experiment simply showed that the speed of light never changes. This idea contradicted Newton's ideas about motion, and it certainly didn't make sense in relation to normal events on Earth.

For example, imagine you're in a car traveling 30 miles per hour. Another car begins to pass you traveling 40 miles per hour. Someone standing on the side of the road sees the second car speed by at 40 miles per hour, but because you're in motion, it appears to be moving only 10 miles per hour.

Now imagine that the second car is a beam of light. According to Einstein, whether that beam of light is measured by the person standing still, by you in the car traveling at 30 miles per hour, or by someone in a space shuttle zipping along at 17,000 miles per hour, its speed will be the same to all three of you.

In 1905, Einstein published his Special Theory of Relativity. He stated that the speed of light is a **constant** and is the top speed in the universe—nothing can move more quickly. Anything with mass can't even come close.

The impact of Einstein's paper wasn't immediately recognized, but eventually other scientists saw that Newton's laws break down when matter approaches the speed of light. One hundred years later, physicists are still making discoveries based on Einstein's theories.

Circle the letter of the best answer to each question below.

1. Einstein's Special Theory of Relativity showed that

    a. Newton's laws were no longer valid.

    b. light waves travel through an invisible medium.

    c. the speed of light is relative.

    d. matter cannot travel at the speed of light.

2. The letters in the equation $E=MC^2$ stand for

    a. entropy, motion, and constant.

    b. energy, mass, and the speed of light.

    c. energy, matter, and the speed of light.

    d. energy, mass, and time.

Write your answers on the lines below.

3. Earth speeds along at more than 66,000 miles per hour as it circles the sun. How does this motion affect the speed of light emitted by the sun?

    _____

4. Why do Newton's laws of motion and gravity still apply to the movements of planets and other objects around the sun?

    _____

Unifying Concepts and Processes

Nothing with mass can travel anywhere close to the speed of light. Light is a wave, but it's also particles of energy called photons. Why are these particles capable of traveling at the speed of light?

_____

What's Next?

Albert Einstein was one science's most brilliant minds, but he was also a fascinating individual. Look for a biography of Einstein's life in the library, and learn more about his role in developing nuclear energy and his opposition to nuclear weapons.

Circle the letter of the best answer to each question below.

1. What is a genome?

    a. a single fragment of a gene

    b. a chemical contained in DNA

    c. a base pair found in genes

    d. an organism's entire genetic code

2. Most historians consider the earliest example of software to be

    a. the punch cards used in Jacquard's loom.

    b. the "calculating clock" invented by Wilhelm Schickard.

    c. integrated circuits used in calculators.

    d. microprocessors.

3. Otto Hahn and Lise Meitner discovered nuclear fission when they were

    a. bombarding nuclei with neutrons.

    b. creating isotopes.

    c. trying to create an atomic bomb.

    d. experimenting with quarks.

Write your answers on the lines below.

4. What effect did Jacques Cousteau's films have on the public?

   _____

5. How does the selection about the Clovis people demonstrate how scientific knowledge can change over time?

   _____

   _____

6. What evidence have archaeologists found that shows ancient Americans had an understanding of at least some astronomical events?

   _____

7. List two scientific or technological events that enabled scientists to complete the Human Genome Project.

   _____   _____

8. How did Eli Whitney's invention affect Southern farmers?

   _____

9. Which two pieces of technology allowed for the miniaturization of computers?

   _____

10. Why didn't Lise Meitner join the other scientists who took part in the Manhattan Project?

   _____

11. Why were space shuttles more practical and economical than earlier manned space vehicles?

   _____

12. Do the risks of space travel outweigh the benefits? Why?

   _____

13. Describe one of the ideas introduced in Einstein's Special Theory of Relativity.

   _____

14. How did Einstein's theory affect Newton's laws of motion?

   _____

Match each term in column 1 with its description in column 2. Write the letter of your answer on the line.

15. _____ Aqua-Lung   a. one of two days each year when day and night are equal lengths

16. _____ medium   b. a device used to calculate numbers

17. _____ algorithm   c. the equipment a shuttle carries into space

18. _____ equinox   d. a substance through which a force or an effect can travel

19. _____ solstice   e. an early version of SCUBA diving equipment

20. _____ abacus   f. a series of instructions, usually leading to a mathematical solution

21. _____ payload   g. either the shortest or longest day of the year

Use the words in the box to complete the sentences below.

reactive	constant	interpretation	olfactory	endorphins
litmus	relative	niche	eradicate	absolute
indicator	cohesive	genome	forensic	mitosis

1. The Burgess Shale fossils were determined to be from the Cambrian Explosion because of the presence of trilobite fossils. This is an example of _____ dating.

2. Radiometric dating was used to determine that the Clovis culture existed about 13,000 years ago. This is an example of _____ dating.

3. Elements that are close to having full outer orbitals tend to be highly _____.

4. _____ paper is used to test a substance's acidity.

5. The _____ force holds the molecules of substances together and is responsible for surface tension.

6. Cells reproduce through a process called _____.

7. Our sense of smell is controlled by millions of _____ neurons located behind the nose.

8. Frogs are an example of a(n) _____ species because their population levels can provide data about the health of an ecosystem.

9. A species will develop its own sound _____ in order to communicate clearly.

10. _____ plays a big role in how meteorologists predict the weather.

11. Investigators use _____ science to solve crimes.

12. Exercising releases _____, which help alleviate feelings of stress.

13. WHO's goal is to _____ many modern diseases by educating people and immunizing them.

14. A _____ is the entire sequence of an organism's DNA.

15. The speed of light is a _____.

Write **true** or **false** next to each statement below.

16. _____ The skin color of many dinosaurs is determined from DNA evidence.

17. _____ Cicada broods can be destroyed by human development.

18. _____ Scientists are unsure whether humans are contributing to climate change.

19. _____ Gravity is the weakest of the four fundamental forces.

20. _____ The brain is like a muscle because it can physically grow and change with use.

21. _____ Natural selection is based on the idea that only the biggest and strongest members of a species will survive.

22. _____ A geyser can form wherever hot water reaches Earth's surface.

23. _____ River deltas are formed by the buildup of sediment.

24. _____ The Mediterranean Sea is the largest remnant of the ancient Tethys Sea.

25. _____ Scientists didn't spot the first exoplanet through a telescope until the 1990s.

26. _____ Our sun is a red giant star that creates energy through nuclear fusion.

27. _____ Binary numbers consist only of 0s and 1s.

28. _____ All televisions create images from electrical signals.

29. _____ Research and education are two of the FDA's responsibilities.

30. _____ Space junk that reenters Earth's atmosphere rarely burns up.

31. _____ Hydrocarbons are one of the biggest threats to animals following an oil spill.

32. _____ Ancient American astronomers understood that Earth traveled around the sun.

33. _____ Space shuttles are one of the most technologically complex machines ever built.

Write your answers on the lines below.

34. Is most science based on inductive or deductive reasoning? Explain your answer.

_____

35. Choose one discovery or invention that was discussed in this book and describe how ethics played a role in its development or plays a role in its use.

_____

_____

36. What is the difference between electrical conduction and electrical induction?

_____

_____

37. What causes an atom to emit photons?

_____

_____

38. How is plasma different from the other states of matter?

_____

39. Explain in detail why ice floats.

_____

_____

40. What is the difference between diffusion and osmosis?

_____

_____

41. What do ice core layers contain that scientists can use to study Earth's atmosphere?

_____

42. Choose one type of rock, and describe how it's formed.

_____

_____

43. Why are black holes invisible?

_____

44. What is biotechnology?

_____

45. How did the use of transistors change electronic devices?

_____

46. Maglev technology uses the fundamental force of _____ to overpower the

fundamental force of _____.

47. How does the International Space Station get the energy it needs to function?

_____

48. Which types of foods should an athlete eat, and which ones should he or she avoid, before a
competition?

_____

49. What effect do pesticides have on the environment?

_____

50. What was the cause of the nuclear power disaster in Chernobyl?

_____

51. How did scientists' ideas about the Clovis people change over time?

_____

Match each scientist with his or her discovery or invention. Write the letter of your choice on the line.

52. _____ Louis Pasteur   **a.** inventor of the Aqua-Lung

53. _____ Michael Faraday   **b.** discovered electromagnetic induction

54. _____ Charles Darwin   **c.** promoted the idea that microorganisms cause disease

55. _____ Albert Einstein   **d.** helped discover nuclear fission

56. _____ Jacques Cousteau   **e.** developed the theory of natural selection

57. _____ Lise Meitner   **f.** the inventor of the cotton gin

58. _____ Eli Whitney   **g.** developed the theories of special and general relativity

Page 7

1. deductive
2. deductive
3. inductive
4. inductive
5. inductive
6. Answers will vary.
7. Answers will vary.

Page 9

1. true
2. false
3. false
4. true
5. true
6. Possible answer: They could also have had characteristics that scientists would have no way of knowing about.
7. They can use CT scans, as well as computers to make 3-D models of the dinosaurs' skulls.
8. Paleontologists believe that dinosaurs were probably colored to blend in to their environments, so knowing what the environment looked like can help scientists make an educated guess about the dinosaurs' coloring.
9. Possible answer: If they were colorblind, then they probably wouldn't have had protective coloring. They might have had colors very different than how we picture them today.
10. Possible answer: It can give them information about how the bones fit together, as well as give them clues about how muscles and tendons filled out the body.

Page 11

1. d
2. c
3. Possible answer: No. Although the Burgess Shale fossils didn't support the hypothesis, other evidence might.
4. Possible answer: Scientists might not understand a piece of archeological evidence when it's first found, but after other evidence or knowledge is gained, the artifact can be reexamined and better understood at that point.
5. Possible answer: In science, anything stated to be true must be supported by careful research and evidence. If sloppy or inexact methods were used, the statement's truthfulness must remain in doubt.

Page 13

1. Possible answer: An earthquake might disturb the original arrangement of layers.
2. Marcus   Amira   Lea   Sam
3. Possible answer: Relative dating allows you to arrange the friends in order by age. Absolute dating can't be used because not enough information is given to find their actual ages.
4. Possible answer: The known rate of decay allows you to measure how much of the element remains in the fossil or artifact in order to determine how old it is.
5. It can only be used to date things that are less than about 40,000 years old.

6. Possible answer: A paleontologist finds a fossil. She uses carbon dating (an absolute method) to determine that the fossil is about 25,000 years old. She also uses the law of superposition (a relative method) with other fossils found in the same bed to confirm her findings.

Unifying Concepts and Processes

relative dating

Page 15

1. *Tibicen* cicadas spend only about three years underground as nymphs, while *Magicicadas* spend 13 or 17 years underground.

2. Cicadas emerge from the ground as nymphs, climb into trees, and molt. The adults mate, and then the males die. Females lay eggs in branches, and then they die. The eggs hatch a few weeks later, the larvae fall to the ground, and they burrow back underground until they emerge as nymphs.

3. Possible answer: When they all die, the millions of dead bugs add nutrients to the soil.

4. Possible answer: Predators can't possibly eat that many cicadas at once, so the species can survive.

5. Possible answer: At one time, there may have been cicadas there, but trees were cut down and the soil was dug up for development. This destroyed the cicadas' habitat and killed the nymphs in the ground. Even if trees grew back in these suburban areas, cicadas don't migrate, so new cicadas didn't move back there.

Page 17

1. b

2. a

3. d

4. It is the idea that microorganisms cause disease. It took a long time to gain acceptance because scientists didn't believe that something so small could have much of an effect on a human being.

5. Possible answer: Pasteur didn't mean to heat the cholera cultures—it happened by accident. If he hadn't been observant, he wouldn't have made his discovery.

6. Pasteurization is the use of heat to kill microorganisms in beverages like milk and juice.

Page 19

1. 50

2. 32

3. 118

4. Because one tree may be larger than another, even if it is not as tall.

5. Possible answer: So they can see how the environment affects trees and so that they can try to help preserve the largest, healthiest tress in a species.

6. Possible answers: acid rain, deforestation, disease

7. Possible answer: Because each species is different and will achieve different maximum sizes.

Page 21

1. autonomy

2. Possible answer: People have to confront possibilities that didn't exist before. Gene therapy and life-support machines are two examples.

3. They are worried about how it might be used in the future. For example, it could be used to eliminate certain "undesirable" traits from a population.

4. Answers will vary.

5. Possible answer: Many people want to keep their health issues private. If a doctor shared medical information, it could affect a person's private or professional life.

6. Possible answer: Stem cells could be used to treat serious diseases. Some people believe that human beings don't have a right to use these cells.

Page 23

1. d

2. Possible answer: ice core samples, increase in average temperatures worldwide, rise in sea levels, movement of animals toward poles

3. Greenhouse gases create a sort of blanket in Earth's atmosphere that holds in too much of the sun's heat and causes temperatures to rise.

4. Because temperatures where they live are rising and causing changes to their ecosystems and environment.

5. Possible answer: The rise in temperatures wasn't very dramatic. People might have been frightened or not have wanted to make changes in their lifestyles.

Page 24

1. d

2. b

3. b

4. a

5. Deductive reasoning uses broad, general truths to draw conclusions about specific facts or events. Inductive reasoning uses specific facts or events to draw conclusions about broader truths.

6. If it is tested repeatedly and never disproved, it becomes a theory. If a theory is never proven wrong over a period of time, it might become a law.

Page 25

7. The presence of trilobite fossils did, because scientists already knew trilobites were part of the Cambrian Explosion.

8. If the ground is disturbed, the nymphs can be destroyed. If trees are cut down, the nymphs have no roots to feed on or branches to molt in.

9. Relative dating tells how old things are in relation to one another. The law of superposition is one example. Absolute dating gives an actual age. Radiometric dating is an example.

10. girth, height, circumference

11. People are concerned that it could be used to eliminate certain "undesirable" traits from a population.

12. worldwide rise in temperatures, rise in sea levels, melting polar ice caps

13. true

14. false

15. false

16. true

17. true

18. false

Page 27

1. d

2. c

3. Electrical conduction occurs when two conductive substances are touching and the current can move from one into the other. Induction is when a changing magnetic field causes an electrical current in a conductive substance.

4. Possible answer: The magnetized needle should move toward the current, because it is attracted to the magnetic field surrounding the current.

Unifying Concepts and Processes

Possible answer: A force is energy that can cause change. An electromagnetic field can induce electrical currents or attract magnetized objects, so it's a force.

Page 29

1. c

2. b

3. a

4. 2; 6

5. 2; 8; 3

6. 2; 8; 1

Page 31

1. a

2. c

3. d

4. As an excited electron returns to its original orbital, it emits a photon.

Unifying Concepts and Processes

1. Possible answers: They both move through space as waves. They both have photons of energy.

2. Possible answer: It has to have enough extra energy in order to emit electromagnetic energy. Also, it will eventually run out of this extra energy and stop producing light.

Page 33

1. c

2. c

3. weak

4. gravity

5. strong

6. electromagnetic

7. photons

8. gluons

9. gravitons

10. Possible answer: All matter has either potential or kinetic energy, but that energy isn't a force unless it's causing changes in the shape or movement of matter.

Page 35

1. a
2. b
3. c
4. solid, liquid, gas, plasma
5. Possible answer: The gas inside a fluorescent tube becomes plasma when an electrical current is added and the energized atoms emit photons.

Unifying Concepts and Processes

Possible answer: It's more like a fluorescent light. Neon is a gas, and a neon light contains this gas in a tube. When electricity is added, it changes to plasma and emits light.

Page 37

1. d
2. a
3. Possible answer: She could add something basic to it, like baking soda. She could keep testing it using litmus paper until she got a reading of 7.
4. Possible answer: You could use only a small amount of water, or you could let some of the liquid boil away to leave behind a more concentrated solution.
5. The distilled water is pure, so it would have a neutral pH. Tap water might not be completely neutral.
6. Yes, but it would need to contain anthocyanin pigments.

Page 39

1. b
2. The molecules are more attracted to each other than to the surrounding air.
3. Possible answer: Weight. An extremely dense object that's very tiny, and therefore has little weight, won't have enough gravitational force to break through the surface tension.
4. Possible answer: As the heat rises, the increasingly rapid motion of the molecules weakens the cohesive forces. Steam is water molecules that have overcome cohesion enough to drift away.

Unifying Concepts and Properties

the electromagnetic force

Page 41

1. d
2. c
3. Because the molecules in ice are bonded in a way that leaves more space between them than the molecules in liquid water.
4. Possible answer: The floating ice displaced an amount of water equal to it in weight. Once it melted, though, the water level didn't change because the volume of water added to the glass didn't change.

Unifying Concepts and Processes

Possible answer: More of the iceberg will be visible in saltwater. Saltwater is denser, so it weighs more. The floating ice displaces less total saltwater than freshwater, so it doesn't sink as far down into the salt water.

Page 43

1. a

2. Possible answer: water with blue food coloring, 70% isopropyl alcohol, 90% isopropyl alcohol with red food coloring

3. Possible answer: Substances that are less dense will float on the surface of denser substances. The order of the layers means that each substance floats on the substance below it.

4. Possible answer: Yes. As long as the liquids are added carefully and don't break the surface tension, it acts as an additional barrier to keep the liquids from mixing.

5. Possible answer: A penny is denser than water, so it is also denser than the other liquids in the column. The penny would sink through all the layers to the bottom of the container.

Page 44

1. c

2. d

3. a

4. Conduction

5. Induction

6. Groups have the same number of electrons in their outermost shells. Periods have the same total number of shells.

7. The visible spectrum is the range of visible light waves and is one small part of the electromagnetic spectrum, which is the entire range of electromagnetic wavelengths.

Page 45

8. When an energized electron falls back to its original orbital, it releases a photon of energy.

9. gravity, weak, electromagnetic, strong

10. strong, weak, gravity, electromagnetic

11. Plasma and gas are structurally similar, but plasma is made up of ions and free electrons.

12. Possible answers: lightning, aurora borealis, a plasma TV

13. Because red cabbage contains anthocyanin pigments and lettuce does not.

14. When liquid water solidifies, the molecules form a crystal structure that increases the amount of space between molecules. Ice is less dense than liquid water, so it will float.

15. They have positive and negative ends.

16. inert

17. semiconductor

18. gluon

19. neutral

20. cohesion

Page 47

1. centromere

2. interphase

3. nuclear

4. cytokinesis

5. centrosomes

6. mitosis

7. chromatin

8. DNA

9. chromosomes

10. cell

11. They transport the identical sets of chromosomes to each side of the cell, and they push the cell apart.

Unifying Concepts and Processes

Possible answer: The DNA is most likely to be abnormal because it contains the information that tells the cell what to do.

Page 49

1. false

2. true

3. false

4. false

5. true

6. The Tibetan monks had spent thousands of hours meditating, while the control group had just learned how.

7. So that scientists could compare the experimental group to it and see what the effects of long-term, expert mediation are on the brain

8. Possible answer: It means that we can keep improving our brains and making them stronger throughout our lifetimes. Someone who has a stroke or head injury has a greater chance of recovery because other portions of the brain can take over for the damaged parts.

9. Possible answer: Because the part of the brain that used to be responsible for interpreting touch in the limb has a new purpose and now interprets touch on the face

10. They were surprised that the brains of the people who only thought about practicing also changed. They concluded that thoughts have the ability to change the structure of the brain.

Page 51

1. b

2. a

3. solutes, solvents

4. Possible answer: The solution outside of the potato had a higher concentration of solutes than inside the potato. Osmosis caused water to move out of the potato to equalize the concentrations in both areas.

5. Possible answer: The pure water outside of the potato had a much lower concentration of solutes than inside the potato. Osmosis caused water to move into the potato to equalize the concentrations.

Page 53

1. cilia

2. Olfaction

3. molecules

4. genes

5. nasal cavity

6. Examples will vary. The limbic system includes the parts of the brain that are linked to memory and emotion.

7. Possible answer: It can be involved in sensing danger, mating, and finding food.

8. Taste buds recognize only sweet, sour, bitter, and salty flavors. About 75% of what you interpret as taste comes from your sense of smell.

Unifying Concepts and Processes

Possible answer: Sense of smell is probably less important today than it was long ago. For example, we have refrigeration so foods don't spoil as quickly, and when they do, we have easy access to other foods. We are also not as in-tune with our environment as we used to be. We rely on things other than our senses to tell as about our environments.

Page 55

1. false

2. false

3. true

4. false

5. true

6. Answers will vary.

7. Amphibians live both in the water and on land. In addition, they are extra-sensitive to changes in their environment because they have porous skin and eggs.

8. They can see whether or not the breeding patterns changed, which would indicate changes in the environment.

9. Additive causes are the combined effects of two or more factors.

Unifying Concepts and Processes

Possible answer: Scientists collect data and pieces of information about the indicator species. Then, they use this information to come to more general conclusions about the environment and the species' ecosystem.

Page 57

1. a

2. b

3. It means that organisms that are best suited to their environment survive, reproduce, and pass along their traits to future generations.

4. Possible answer: The 13 species of finches on the islands evolved from one ancestor with beaks that were suited to the food on the specific island where they lived.

5. Possible answers: global warming and land development

Unifying Concepts and Processes

Possible answer: The members of the native species that were best able to deal with the competition from the invasive species would have the best chances of surviving and reproducing. Natural selection would take place, and the "fittest" of the native species would become the majority.

Page 59

1. d

2. Bioluminescence generates a light that gives off almost no heat, while a light bulb wastes most of its energy in heat. The light of bioluminescence is produced chemically.

3. luciferin, luciferase, oxygen

4. Possible answers: Bioluminescence is used by glowworms to attract prey. It is used by the brittle star to repel predators.

5. Possible answer: Because it is useful for their success in surviving and breeding

Page 61

1. false

2. true

3. false

4. false

5. true

6. Possible answer: Pickleweed stores salt in a vacuole that falls off once it becomes full.

7. Possible answer: Because most plants do not have adaptations that allow them to live in a salty environment

8. They help prevent erosion and flooding and shield the area near the coast from the effects of severe storms.

9. There is a lot of available food, and the tall grasses keep them protected from predators.

10. Possible answer: The tide washes in and out of salt marshes, which sweeps away dead plant life and brings in fresh nutrients.

11. Possible answer: Marshes used to be dredged to create shipping channels or filled in to create more oceanfront land. Today, they are more valued and protected.

Page 63

1. c

2. He wants to preserve them before they disappear. He also wants to bring people's attention to what we may be losing.

3. He can find an audio signature for each type of animal at a different frequency.

4. Possible answer: Animals find a unique sound niche in which to make their sounds to ensure that they will be heard by others of their species.

5. loss of habitat, human activity, human development

6. Possible answer: It can block out the sounds of animals. This can make it difficult for marine mammals to communicate. It can also keep frogs from chirping in harmony, which makes them more vulnerable to predators.

Unifying Concepts and Processes

Possible answer: Animals that find their own sound space may have a better chance of surviving and breeding. According to the laws of natural selection, as evolution takes place, these animals will replace the others of their species that didn't find a unique sound niche.

Page 64

1. c

2. b

3. a

4. Neuroplasticity is the ability of the human brain to physically change in response to thoughts and experiences. This is especially significant to people who have had a stroke or a head injury.

5. Possible answers: pleasure and to determine if food is spoiled; to find food and to find a mate

6. Taste buds recognize only sweet, sour, bitter, and salty flavors. About 75% of what you interpret as taste comes from your sense of smell.

7. Amphibians live both in the water and on land. In addition, they are extra-sensitive to changes in their environment because they have porous skin and eggs.

Page 65

8. 6, 4, 5, 1, 2, 3

9. Possible answer: Animals find a unique sound niche in which to make their sounds to ensure that they will be heard by others of their species.

10. Possible answer: It can serve as a method of self-defense, a way of finding a mate, or a way to attract prey. The firefly uses it to attract a mate.

11. The light gray gyspy moth used to have an advantage because it blended in with its surroundings. When the Industrial Revolution took place, everything was covered in soot and the dark gray moth had better protective coloring. Through natural selection, it evolved to become the majority.

12. New research indicates that the brains of adult human beings are (fixed, <u>changeable</u>).

13. A cell spends the majority of its life in (<u>interphase</u>, cytokinesis).

14. (<u>Osmosis</u>, Diffusion) is when the solvent in a solution with low concentration flows toward a solution with high concentration.

15. Cilia are hair-like structures that contain odor-sensitive (neurons, <u>receptors</u>).

16. Breeding a species of plant that is resistant to disease is an example of (natural, <u>artificial</u>) selection.

Page 66

1. false

2. true

3. true

4. false

5. false

6. false

7. false

8. true

9. girth

10. physiology

11. photons

12. messenger particles

13. Plasmas

14. chromosomes; centromeres

15. semi-permeable

16. Cilia

Page 67

17. spontaneous

18. To make sure that their conclusions support one another and are correct

19. inductive

20. We need greenhouse gases to make the planet warm enough to support life. Too many greenhouse gases in the atmosphere, though, can cause temperatures to rise.

21. He induced an electrical current in the wire.

22. Their outermost electron shells are full, so they are seldom reactive.

23. Water molecules are more attracted to each other than the table because of cohesion.

24. crystal

25. Neuroplasticity is the ability of the human brain to physically change in response to thoughts and experiences.

26. The solutes in a highly concentrated solution will move toward a solution with a lower concentration of solutes.

27. They alerted human beings to the fact that DDT was harmful to the environment and to living creatures.

Page 69

1. a

2. c

3. d

4. Possible answer: Because everyone starts out with the same set of facts, but the accuracy of a prediction depends on how they interpret the facts.

5. Because it doesn't work in areas where the weather is changeable or when fronts are moving quickly.

6. Possible answer: A meteorologist has to carefully observe what the current weather is before making a prediction. He or she also needs to closely observe signs that indicate changes in weather.

Page 71

1. c

2. a

3. The polar regions contain a much thicker covering of ice, so the cores can be much longer.

4. The new layers of snow at the surface contain gases and particles from the atmosphere. As new layers fall and these old layers are pushed down, the gases and particles are sealed in with the snow.

5. Possible answer: With each additional layer, the weight pressing down on previous layers increases, so the oldest, deepest layers are much more compressed and harder to read.

Unifying Concepts and Processes

Possible answer: There might be missing information in one of the cores if snow didn't fall in that area. The data is also more reliable if there is evidence from two places.

Page 73

1. b

2. a source of heat, a good supply of water, and an underground constriction

3. groundwater that is the result of precipitation

4. They can sap the water supply.

5. Possible answer: Because if the rocks were porous, they would let out steam and water and there wouldn't be enough pressure to create a geyser

6. Possible answer: It is an area through which water cannot pass easily. A constriction keeps water from easily bubbling out of the earth and creates additional pressure underground.

7. Possible answer: what kind of water supply they have and how long it takes for the plumbing to fill up

Page 75

1. meandering

2. estuary

3. tributaries

4. glaciers

5. delta

6. by building levees

7. Possible answer: It could destroy human development as well as natural habitat if it had a major change in course.

8. It collects rainwater and runoff from snow and accumulates sediment.

9. The Upper Mississippi cuts through hilly terrain and high bluffs. The Lower Mississippi flows through flatter land, is deeper, carries more water, and has a more powerful current.

10. The delta was formed when sea levels rose and the glaciers retreated. The marshy coastline of Louisiana was created by the river's deposits of alluvium.

11. It helps absorb the impact from severe weather and is a defense against flooding.

Page 77

1. a

2. denser

3. the remains of living organisms

4. Possible answer: Intrusive rocks are coarse, while extrusive rocks are usually smooth.

5. erosion; the movement of tectonic plates

6. Weathering breaks rocks down into smaller pieces.

Unifying Concepts and Processes

Possible answer: If there is any effect, it is minimal. The rock cycle happens on a geological time scale that is much longer than the time human beings have even existed on Earth.

Page 79

1. d

2. c

3. The continents are part of tectonic plates that move over, under, and alongside each other.

4. As water evaporates from the sea's surface, the seawater becomes more concentrated. Because the Mediterranean is almost entirely enclosed by land, less concentrated saltwater doesn't readily mix back in.

5. Because it's the location where two of Earth's tectonic plates meet.

Unifying Concepts and Processes

Possible answer: In order for an object to float, it must be less dense than the liquid it's placed in. The high concentration of salt in the Dead Sea makes the water denser than water in other places, so objects are even more likely to float there.

Answer Key

Page 81

1. d

2. Possible answer: An exoplanet's size can be determined by how much the star dims, and its orbital speed can be determined by how long the dimming lasts.

3. Star A's habitable zone would be farther away, because if it was closer or in the same place, water would be a gas, not a liquid.

Unifying Concepts and Processes

Possible answer: Stars emit light because they are intensely hot plasmas with excited, photon-emitting electrons. Planets are cooler solids, liquids, or gases that might reflect some light, but don't produce much on their own.

Page 83

1. b

2. a

3. 2, 5, 3, 1, 4

4. Possible answer: Supernova and planetary nebula are the stages in a star's life when it gives off dust and particles. Eventually, the dust and particles could become part of a nebula and begin a new star.

Unifying Concepts and Processes

Different wavelengths of color have different amounts of energy, starting with red as the lowest and increasing through the spectrum.

Page 85

1. b

2. c

3. Because they don't reflect electromagnetic radiation.

4. Possible answer: Mass is a measure of how much matter an object contains, not its size. Black holes contain incredible amounts of mass, but they can be as small as atoms.

5. Possible answer: Black holes are the most massive objects in the universe, and smaller masses always orbit larger masses.

6. Possible answer: Neither, because hot and cold are measures of temperature, and there is no way to measure a black hole's temperature.

Page 86

1. a

2. c

3. d

4. Possible answer: Meteorologists usually have the same raw data to work with. Their forecasts depend on how they interpret that data.

5. Because different kinds of snow fall in summer than in winter.

6. a source of heat, a supply of water, and a constriction

7. retreating glaciers

8. Because it is located where two tectonic plates meet.

Page 87

9. Igneous rocks are formed when magma cools. Sedimentary rocks are formed when layers of sediment are compressed together.

10. the area surrounding a star that is the perfect distance from the star so that water can be a liquid

11. Possible answer: The astronomer can search for stars that dim at regular intervals.

12. gravity

13. They can't be seen because they don't reflect any electromagnetic radiation.

14. The object will be sucked into the black hole due to the intense gravitational force.

15. persistence

16. glacial

17. estuary

18. magma

19. tectonic

20. luminous

21. sequence

Page 89

1. Possible answers: saliva or tooth imprints from the leftover food; hair samples from where he leaned on the couch; skin, hair, and possibly even blood samples from the razor he shaved with; fingerprints from the refrigerator door or remote control

2. by examining bones and sometimes performing chemical analyses on them

3. Possible answer: Computers allow fingerprints to be recorded and shared. Software allows documents to be traced to specific printers.

4. traces wherever they go

5. Possible answer: by using others sources of evidence in combination with DNA testing

Page 91

1. biodiversity

2. Cloning

3. fermentation

4. biodegradable

5. Because human beings use the plants to create a product that has desirable characteristics.

6. The Frozen Ark is a DNA bank. Its purpose is to preserve the genetic material of animals that are threatened with extinction.

7. Bioremediation is the use of living organisms to break down toxic materials in the environment.

8. Possible answer: Because evolution happens naturally; it's not controlled by human beings.

Page 93

1. c

2. c

3. They don't have to overcome friction to move, and they don't need engines.

4. Possible answer: They don't need to be connected because the entire train moves as a unit; there isn't just a single engine at the front pulling all the other cars.

5. Possible answer: The noise of a maglev train comes from the train pushing through air. The faster it goes, the bigger the sound waves it creates, and the noisier it is.

Unifying Concepts and Processes

Possible answer: No, because the electromagnetic force has already overcome gravity and gravity doesn't become stronger just because the train is moving uphill.

Page 95

1. b

2. a

3. Possible answer: Analog information, because our sensations of the world aren't broken up into small, distinct pieces that we have to put back together. We experience the world as a whole.

4. Possible answer: Yes, because light, sound, or radio waves can be turned off and on to create sequences in the same way electrical pulses are.

Page 97

1. b

2. c

3. Transistors are smaller, don't generate much heat, and are more reliable.

4. Because they can act like either insulators or conductors.

5. Possible answer: As transistors became smaller and more powerful, electronic devices that used them could also be made smaller and could run off low-power batteries.

Unifying Concepts and Processes

Possible answer: If there is air in the tube, the electrons would run into the atoms in the air and not go wherever they needed to go.

Page 99

1. c

2. d

3. The alternator doesn't generate electricity until the motor is running, so the battery provides the initial spark to start the motor.

4. A jet engine allows the combusting gases to flow out of the cylinder instead of trapping them. The gases shooting out the back propel the jet forward.

Unifying Concepts and Processes

1. induction

2. Possible answer: When fuel and air are drawn into the cylinder, they have potential chemical energy. The spark creates combustion, and this potential energy turns into kinetic energy that forces the piston down. The piston's kinetic energy is transferred to the gears and other pistons, giving them kinetic energy as well.

Page 101

1. false

2. true

3. true

4. false

5. true

6. Predators use camouflage so that their prey doesn't see them approaching. Prey use camouflage as a defense against predators.

7. Possible answer: In an optical illusion, the brain can't perceive the reality of what the eyes are seeing because of a visual "trick," such as camouflage.

8. Camouflage develops through natural selection because it gives animals a better chance at survival, which makes them more likely to live long enough to reproduce.

9. Possible answer: a leopard

10. They are pigment cells that allow certain animals to change their skin color.

11. It is often used as a form of disguise in hunting and warfare.

12. It keeps lions from being able to pick out individual zebras in the herd.

Page 103

1. b

2. c

3. b

4. It was an all-electrical system.

Unifying Concepts and Processes

The electrical signals have to be converted into signals carried by a radio wave.

Page 105

1. c

2. c

3. The ISS is expensive and difficult to construct. A larger, better station can be built by working together.

4. Because it would be impossible to launch the finished station into space.

5. to provide living quarters

6. Possible answers: experimentation and observation in the fields of biology, physics, chemistry, astronomy, and meteorology; Microgravity makes space an interesting place to conduct scientific investigations.

Page 106

1. c

2. a

3. d

4. d

5. Possible answer: A forensic anthropologist studies and analyzes bones to learn basic information about a person, such as his or her height, gender, and ethnicity, as well as information about what type of life the person led.

6. Because DNA is unique to individuals, it can provide investigators with a reliable means of identification.

Page 107

7. The Frozen Ark is a DNA bank. Its purpose is to preserve the genetic material of animals that are threatened with extinction.

8. They don't have to overcome friction, and they don't use engines.

9. It has to be broken up into small, distinct pieces that can each be assigned a code.

10. Because transistors are smaller, don't create as much heat, and are more reliable.

11. Possible answer: In an optical illusion, the brain can't perceive the reality of what the eyes are seeing because of a visual "trick," such as camouflage.

12. a substance with conductivity that's affected by light

13. The ISS is being constructed piece by piece in space because it would be impossible to launch the entire station if it were constructed on Earth.

14. Biotechnology plays an important role in the creation of (<u>biodegradable</u>, transgenic) materials that are less damaging to the environment.

15. Maglev trains use (<u>electromagnetic</u>, gravitational) forces to float above their tracks.

16. Computers analyze digital information written as a (electronic, <u>binary</u>) number system.

17. Silicon is the most common (insulator, <u>semiconductor</u>) used in electronic devices.

18. A car engine's alternator (<u>induces</u>, conduces) an electrical current that can be used for combustion.

19. A (<u>piston</u>, gear) moves up and down inside each cylinder of an internal combustion engine.

20. Philo Farnsworth invented the first all (mechanical, <u>electrical</u>) television system.

Page 109

1. c

2. Possible answers: my grades in math, my parents' divorce, my grandpa's health

3. "Fight or flight" is the body's physical reaction to a situation of stress or danger. It's an instinctual response that prepares you to deal with the situation by fighting or fleeing.

4. Possible answer: I had an argument with my sister, and we didn't talk for a couple of days. I wrote her a letter explaining how I felt, which led to us talking and working things out.

5. Possible answer: take the dog for a walk, listen to my music, go swimming

6. It makes you feel good about yourself and releases endorphins.

7. It can motivate you to work harder.

8. Possible answer: Your best friend moves away. You can't change the situation, but instead of being depressed about it, you could figure out ways to stay in touch and remain close.

Page 111

1. false

2. false

3. true

4. false

5. hydrated

6. supplements

7. protein

8. glycogen

9. because your body gets different nutrients and benefits from different foods

10. It replenishes the water you lose while exercising, but it also replenishes substances like sodium and potassium that you lose when you sweat.

11. Possible answer: whole-wheat spaghetti with tomato sauce, a dinner roll, a glass of water, and an orange; the pasta and bread are a source of carbohydrates, the water hydrates you, and the orange provides a slight sugar boost.

12. Possible answer: They take longer to digest, so your body has to work a little harder. They also make you feel full longer.

Page 113

1. to ensure the safety and quality of foods and drugs

2. A recall occurs when a manufacturer alerts customers that one of its products was defective or harmful in some way and should not be used.

3. Possible answer: Education is important because it can prevent problems from occurring. For example, most cases of food-borne illnesses could be avoided with proper food handling and storage.

4. an additive

5. Possible answers: pharmaceutical drugs, cosmetics, medical devices

6. Possible answer: Yes, they should have been testing more of the foods to make sure that they were safe and didn't contain anything harmful.

7. Possible answer: Human beings and animals are both part of the food chain. If animals like pigs, cows, and fish consume something harmful, it could also affect the human beings who eat those animal products.

Page 115

1. false

2. true

3. false

4. false

5. true

6. Many synthetic fabrics are made from petroleum, a fossil fuel.

7. Possible answer: About a quarter of the pesticides used in the United States are applied to cotton crops, so growing cotton is actually somewhat harmful to the environment.

8. It doesn't require a lot of pesticides.

9. Answers will vary.

10. Possible answer: It reuses old materials instead of wasting them, and it keeps the use of newer materials to a minimum.

11. The layer closest to the body wicks away moisture. The next layer provides insulation. The outer layer offers protection from water/snow and winds.

Page 117

1. d

2. Possible answer: Agriculture led to people living in more concentrated areas, which meant that diseases could spread more easily.

3. Possible answer: It was the first disease to be eliminated through human effort. It was highly contagious and killed large numbers of people.

4. Possible answer: WHO has found that all these conditions have a direct effect on health. To improve people's health, their living and working conditions have to meet certain standards.

5. Possible answer: It can stop the spread of diseases. It can see the big picture of worldwide health, and it has the power of many nations working together to make changes.

6. They are some of the neediest groups. If their situation improved, it would be an indicator that worldwide health as a whole was probably improving.

7. Education can help prevent diseases from spreading. In the case of AIDS, misinformation was contributing to the increased occurrence of the disease.

Page 119

1. a

2. c

3. Earth's gravity pulls it in.

4. friction

5. Because that would just create many more smaller pieces that can't be tracked.

6. They are part of the growing global communication network.

Page 121

1. Possible answer: Pests can cause enormous financial and food losses, but pesticides are harmful to human beings and the environment.

2. people who have close contact with them, like farmers and farm workers

3. You can wash your produce thoroughly or buy organic produce.

4. Possible answers: They kill beneficial insects, they can become part of the groundwater, and they can cause health problems for human beings.

5. Possible answer: IPM is the use of a variety of methods to control pests. By using alternative sources of control, the amount of chemical pesticides used is reduced.

Unifying Concepts and Processes

Possible answer: Some insects or weeds will be resistant to pesticides. Through the process of natural selection, they will survive and reproduce. They will pass along this trait to future generations, resulting in much larger resistant populations over time.

Page 123

1. b

2. c

3. Hydrocarbons can harm an animal's vision, smell, growth, reproduction, and ability to hunt.

4. Possible answer: Animal populations that are prey for birds, such as insects and fish, were probably affected.

5. Large quantities of oil would take a long time to biodegrade, and in the meantime, much harm could be done to animals and the environment.

Unifying Concepts and Processes

Possible answer: Bioremediation could be used to break down the oil and remove it.

Page 125

1. false

2. true

3. true

4. to contain the remaining radiation and prevent it from leaking into the air

5. It is badly in need of repair or replacement.

6. Possible answer: Cancer can take a long time to develop. Also, there is no way of knowing which cases of cancer were caused by the radiation from Chernobyl.

7. Possible answer: Because few human beings live in the exclusion zone, large numbers of animals have returned to the area. If human beings do come back one day in greater numbers, the animal populations are likely to decrease.

Unifying Concepts and Processes

60 years

Page 126

1. b

2. a

3. d

4. Possible answers: exercise and deep breathing

5. Possible answers: insomnia, headaches, clenching or grinding teeth

6. Supplements can be a source of nutrition, but fresh, whole foods are a better, more complete source for both athletes and non-athletes.

7. to ensure the safety and quality of food, drugs, cosmetics, and some medical products

8. Because there is a strong link between poverty and poor health.

Page 127

9. Possible answers: Some synthetic materials are made of petroleum, a fossil fuel, which has a limited supply. Buying clothes made of recycled materials or materials that don't require pesticides to grow can have a positive impact.

10. It can damage satellites or spacecraft and endanger the lives of astronauts.

11. Possible answers: Pro: Pesticides prevent the loss of crops. Con: They can be harmful to the health of human beings and the environment.

12. Because people are becoming more environmentally conscious and realize the harm that pesticides can cause.

13. The oil spills can cause animals to drown or freeze. The hydrocarbons can affect an animal's senses, as well as its ability to reproduce and hunt.

14. true

15. true

16. false

17. true

18. false

19. true

Answer Key

Page 129

1. d
2. Possible answer: He knew what sorts of devices would be most useful in his work, and he applied his firsthand knowledge of ocean exploration when creating his inventions.
3. Possible answer: The films showed the undersea world to people who would have no knowledge of it otherwise and made them care about the oceans.
4. Possible answer: Both explore unknown parts of the universe. Both require special equipment that is necessary for human survival.
5. Possible answer: People would have the opportunity to do a lot more oceanic research, but their presence could disrupt underwater life. If they created any sort of waste or pollution, it could also harm the deep-sea environment.

Page 131

1. c
2. b
3. Instead of one group arriving in a single event, researchers believe they arrived at different times and by different means.
4. They found the spearheads mixed in with mammoth remains.
5. Evidence was building that the theory was no longer correct because older artifacts had been found.
6. Possible answer: This will allow them to verify that the artifacts are actually older than the Clovis materials, and it will help them support their new hypothesis.

Unifying Concepts and Processes

Possible answer: Deductive reasoning was used to determine that since spearheads were found among mammoth remains they had been used to hunt the mammoths.

Page 133

1. A solstice occurs when the sun is farthest from the equator, and an equinox occurs when the sun is closest to the equator.
2. Small holes allowed sunlight to fall on specific places in the room only during the solstices and equinoxes.
3. Possible answer: Ancient peoples would need to know when it was time to plant crops, prepare for winter, or hunt for specific animals.
4. Possible answer: The solar year was determined by counting the number of days that passed from one solstice to the next.

Unifying Concepts and Processes

relative

Page 135

1. a
2. Without high-speed computers, the billions of pieces of DNA base pairs in the human genome would have taken an extremely long time to analyze.
3. It looks at a short strand of DNA and reads which chemicals are in the base pairs.
4. Both groups wanted to be able to say they mapped the genome first, so they worked extra-hard toward the goal. The competition inspired them to find the fastest methods for analyzing the data.

5. Answers will vary.

Page 137

1. combine

2. interchangeable

3. mechanized

4. efficiently

5. manufacturing

6. It solved the problem of how to quickly and efficiently remove cotton from the bolls.

7. five

8. A drum with hooks on it picks out the seeds as the cotton is passed through.

9. Possible answer: Since there was suddenly a lot of cotton available, technology changed in response. Sewing machines were invented, and factories to make fabric sprang up.

Page 139

1. a

2. b

3. Because they contained information that could be used to control a machine.

4. microchips or integrated circuits; microprocessors

Unifying Concepts and Processes

It has to be translated into digital code.

Page 141

1. c

2. b

3. to develop an atomic bomb before the Nazis did

4. Because she knew there weren't many opportunities there for female scientists.

Unifying Concepts and Processes

When Meitner learned that her discovery would be used to create a bomb, she didn't consider it ethical to use this scientific knowledge to build something that would kill people.

Page 143

1. c

2. d

3. e

4. b

5. a

6. He thought it would revolutionize space transportation and give human beings an important tool for learning about the moon, planets, sun, and stars.

7. They could be used 100 times instead of just once.

8. Possible answers: experiments, repair of satellites, transportation of materials to the ISS

9. Possible answer: Yes, I believe that we will continue to explore space. It is risky, but there is much we don't know about the universe, and human beings are always drawn to the unknown.

Page 145

1. d

2. b

3. it doesn't have any effect on the speed of light

4. Because these objects don't move anywhere near the speed of light.

Unifying Concepts and Processes

because photons don't have mass

Page 146

1. d

2. a

3. a

4. They allowed people to get a glimpse of the deep-sea world, which made them care more about preserving the oceans.

5. Possible answers: An accepted theory was disproved when new information was found and better methods of determining age became available.

6. They have found structures built with knowledge of the movements of astronomical objects.

Page 147

7. supercomputers; DNA sequencers

8. It allowed them to plant much more cotton because they could more quickly separate the seeds.

9. microchips and microprocessors

10. Meitner didn't want to take part in a project with the purpose of building a bomb.

11. because they can be used about 100 times instead of just once

12. Answers will vary.

13. Possible answer: Nothing can travel faster than the speed of light.

14. It showed that Newton's laws don't apply to all situations.

15. e

16. d

17. f

18. a

19. g

20. b

21. c

Page 148

1. relative

2. absolute

3. reactive

4. Litmus

5. cohesive

6. mitosis

7. olfactory

8. indicator

9. niche

10. Interpretation

11. forensic

12. endorphins

13. eradicate

14. genome

15. constant

Page 149

16. false

17. true

18. false

19. true

20. true

21. false

22. false

23. true

24. true

25. false

26. false

27. true

28. true

29. true

30. false

31. true

32. false

33. true

34. Most science is inductive because it uses specific events to draw general conclusions about the universe.

Page 150

35. Answers will vary.

36. Electrical conduction is when a current passes between conductors that must be touching. Induction occurs when a current is produced by a changing electromagnetic field.

37. When an atom gains energy, its electron has jumped to an outer orbital. Energy is released in the form of photons as it returns to its original orbital.

38. Plasma is similar to gas, but the atoms are so energized that they begin to lose electrons.

39. When water freezes, the molecules form a crystal structure that is less dense than liquid water, and objects that

are less dense than water will float.

40. Diffusion is the movement of solutes from a highly concentrated solution to one that is less concentrated. Osmosis is the movement of a solvent from an area with a low concentration of solutes to an area of high concentration.

41. They contain trapped gases and particles from the atmosphere in Earth's past.

42. Igneous rocks form when magma cools. It can happen slowly underground, or it can happen quickly when magma emerges from a volcano.

43. They don't reflect any electromagnetic radiation.

Page 151

44. It is the use of living organisms to create products, solve problems, or do tasks that benefit human beings.

45. Devices could become smaller, more powerful, and have easier portability.

46. electromagnetism; gravity

47. Solar panels harness energy from the sun.

48. An athlete should eat carbohydrates and starchy foods before a competition, while avoiding fatty foods and large amounts of proteins.

49. Possible answer: They can pollute groundwater, affect the life cycles of animals, and cause human beings to become ill.

50. There were problems with the design and operation of the plant.

51. For many years, the Clovis were believed to be the first Americans. Recent evidence has shown that other cultures predated them, but scientists do not yet know who those people were.

52. c

53. b

54. e

55. g

56. a

57. d

58. f